TURBO GENEALOGY

AN INTRODUCTION TO FAMILY HISTORY RESEARCH IN THE INFORMATION AGE

BY
JOHN AND CAROLYN COSGRIFF

Cosgriff, John Cornelius.
    Turbo genealogy : an introduction to family history
research in the information age / by John and Carolyn
Cosgriff.
                    p.   cm.
    Includes bibliographical references and index.
    ISBN 0-916489-66-3 (softcover)
    1. United States—Genealogy—Handbooks, manuals,
etc. 2. Genealogy. 3. Genealogy—Computer
programming. 4. Genealogy—Data processing.
I. Cosgriff, Carolyn H. II. Title.
CS47.C67 1996
929' .1'072073—DC20   96-26239

© 1997 Ancestry Incorporated
Published by Ancestry Incorporated
P.O. Box 476
Salt Lake City, Utah 84110-0476

First printing 1997
10 9 8 7 6 5 4 3 2 1

Printed in the United States of America

Contents

Preface

Many people find genealogy intriguing; most find it difficult as well. Fortunately, some long-standing obstacles to genealogical research are beginning to melt away. In the few years since the previous edition of this book, our dream of faster, more efficient research methods has begun to come true. We are optimistic that continuing progress in computer performance will result in many further improvements.

Therefore, this book has a three-fold purpose. First, it is a genealogical research primer. That is, it outlines the steps and requirements for tracing your family tree. Our goal here is to provide basic instruction that will provide you with a foundation for your research and with the ability to begin analyzing family data. You need no extensive background in genealogy to understand and learn from this primer.

The second purpose of this book is to be a reference that will help you take advantage of today's rich environment of research tools. Recent changes in libraries and computer technology can help your research go forward more quickly and efficiently. This book will teach you, for example, how to search many of the computer-generated databases now available. (We have concentrated on sources that have proven most helpful for family research in the U.S., Canada, and Europe; if you're researching ancestry in other countries or from particular ethnic groups, you may need to consult sources other than those we discuss.)

The book's third purpose is to teach you how to effectively use a personal computer to keep track of your research, communicate with other researchers, and electronically access information from remote sources. Because computer technology and software programs have made genealogical research so much more efficient, we examine the advantages of using the computer as a research tool.

We conclude the book by providing progress notes based on many years of computer genealogy experience. Compiling an electronic research database has taught us that computers can help topple the "brick walls" which almost inevitably beset individual researchers. In seeking ways to climb over, around, and even through these brick walls, our perception of the effective study of genealogy has changed significantly. We're discovering that these brick walls may be more a matter of perception than anything else. Linking individuals and families together as integral parts of their respective and surrounding family tree forests has been easier than anticipated, and allows us to go beyond conventional research methods to resolve complex genealogical questions. As a result, we have been prompted to adopt a new paradigm, "eco-genealogy," whereby computer technology helps us reconstruct family structures more fully, more accurately, and more predictively.

So whatever your current level of genealogical and computer experience, we trust the information and ideas in this book will help your family tree research to flourish!

Acknowledgments

We offer sincere gratitude and credit to several people who helped bring this book about. Kory Meyerink, formerly Publications Coordinator of the Family History Department of The Church of Jesus Christ of Latter-day Saints, tops our list. Without his advice, encouragement, and remarkable critique of our infant first draft, the book would have died. Help from friends and library mentors Bob Turner at Radford University, Virginia, and especially J. Carlyle Parker at California State University, Stanislaus, was likewise crucial in the long mid-stage. Several online friends and associates also generously shared their expertise and help whenever requested. Finally, we feel particularly appreciative of the patience and long-suffering of our children during the many months (eventually stretching into years) that the book required.

Heartfelt appreciation in the area of editing goes to several on the Ancestry staff. Hank Borys helped immensely with our hardware and software chapters; Loretto Szucs likewise with our once-unruly Chapter 8. Ever-cheerful Anne Lemmon, during her tenure as managing editor, had an encouraging way to keep us working past the several times we thought we had finished! Jennifer Tonge and Dayna Shoell, although we never met them, continually amazed us with their abilities to fine-tune our rough thoughts; thanks to their efforts, our present understanding of the field stretches far beyond where we began.

Largely because of the outstanding help of these people, we feel confident that this edition is our most helpful yet. But, of course, the usual caveats apply. Despite our attempts, some mistakes have doubtless slipped through. We would appreciate learning of any that you might come across so that they can be corrected in any future revisions.

Chapter 1

Getting Ready

If you've recently become interested in genealogy, you may need help determining where to start. Follow the four basic steps below to begin uncovering your roots.

Step 1. **ORGANIZE:** Organize family data.

Step 2. **ANALYZE:** Analyze the data to identify patterns and trends that may help you direct your research, to determine additional data that you want to obtain, and to locate possible sources for that data. Analysis is the foundation of a sound research strategy.

Step 3. **PLAN:** Devise a research strategy.

Step 4. **SEARCH:** Use all available resources to accomplish your research goals.

Note that the process is circular; family history research ends only when you stop doing it.

Once you have organized and analyzed existing family data, you have a good chance of succeeding in your record-searching, especially if you use a wide variety of sources to help you to verify the information that you have already collected and to find additional information.

Using Forms to Organize Data

You should begin organizing your data as soon as you begin your research. By using the proper forms, you can record and organize information simultaneously. Starting with the information you already have, fill out a Pedigree chart. Then start a Family Group chart for each couple on the Pedigree chart. Keep these forms current: Each time you find a new piece of information, add it to the appropriate form.

Pedigree Charts

Use Pedigree charts (see Figure 1-1) to trace direct ancestry through several generations. Entry Number 1 is yourself or another whose direct line you wish

Pedigree Chart

No. 1 on this chart is the same as no. _____ on chart no. _____

Chart no. _____

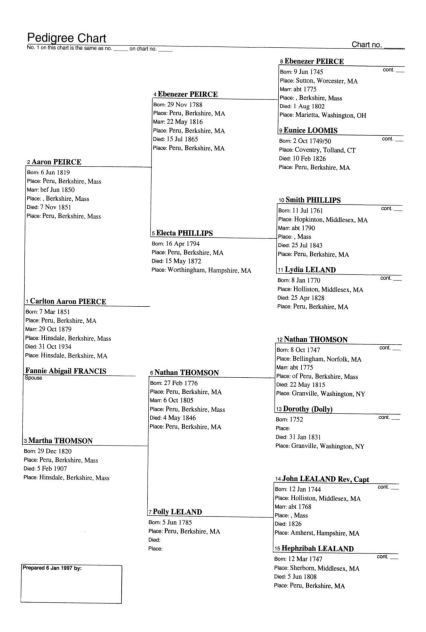

8 Ebenezer PEIRCE
Born: 9 Jun 1745   cont. __
Place: Sutton, Worcester, MA
Marr: abt 1775
Place: , Berkshire, Mass
Died: 1 Aug 1802
Place: Marietta, Washington, OH

9 Eunice LOOMIS
Born: 2 Oct 1749/50   cont. __
Place: Coventry, Tolland, CT
Died: 10 Feb 1826
Place: Peru, Berkshire, MA

4 Ebenezer PEIRCE
Born: 29 Nov 1788
Place: Peru, Berkshire, MA
Marr: 22 May 1816
Place: Peru, Berkshire, MA
Died: 15 Jul 1865
Place: Peru, Berkshire, MA

10 Smith PHILLIPS
Born: 11 Jul 1761   cont. __
Place: Hopkinton, Middlesex, MA
Marr: abt 1790
Place: , Mass
Died: 25 Jul 1843
Place: Peru, Berkshire, MA

11 Lydia LELAND
Born: 8 Jan 1770   cont. __
Place: Holliston, Middlesex, MA
Died: 25 Apr 1828
Place: Peru, Berkshire, MA

5 Electa PHILLIPS
Born: 16 Apr 1794
Place: Peru, Berkshire, MA
Died: 15 May 1872
Place: Worthingham, Hampshire, MA

2 Aaron PEIRCE
Born: 6 Jun 1819
Place: Peru, Berkshire, Mass
Marr: bef Jun 1850
Place: , Berkshire, Mass
Died: 7 Nov 1851
Place: Peru, Berkshire, Mass

1 Carlton Aaron PIERCE
Born: 7 Mar 1851
Place: Peru, Berkshire, MA
Marr: 29 Oct 1879
Place: Hinsdale, Berkshire, Mass
Died: 31 Oct 1934
Place: Hinsdale, Berkshire, MA

Fannie Abigail FRANCIS
Spouse

12 Nathan THOMSON
Born: 8 Oct 1747   cont. __
Place: Bellingham, Norfolk, MA
Marr: abt 1775
Place: of Peru, Berkshire, Mass
Died: 22 May 1815
Place: Granville, Washington, NY

13 Dorothy (Dolly)
Born: 1752   cont. __
Place:
Died: 31 Jan 1831
Place: Granville, Washington, NY

6 Nathan THOMSON
Born: 27 Feb 1776
Place: Peru, Berkshire, MA
Marr: 6 Oct 1805
Place: Peru, Berkshire, Mass
Died: 4 May 1846
Place: Peru, Berkshire, MA

14 John LEALAND Rev, Capt
Born: 12 Jan 1744   cont. __
Place: Holliston, Middlesex, MA
Marr: abt 1768
Place: , Mass
Died: 1826
Place: Amherst, Hampshire, MA

15 Hephzibah LEALAND
Born: 12 Mar 1747   cont. __
Place: Sherborn, Middlesex, MA
Died: 5 Jun 1808
Place: Peru, Berkshire, MA

7 Polly LELAND
Born: 5 Jun 1785
Place: Peru, Berkshire, MA
Died:
Place:

3 Martha THOMSON
Born: 29 Dec 1820
Place: Peru, Berkshire, Mass
Died: 5 Feb 1907
Place: Hinsdale, Berkshire, Mass

Prepared 6 Jan 1997 by:

Figure 1-1. Pedigree Chart

to record. Entry Number 2 is the father of Number 1, and entry Number 3 is the mother. The pattern is used throughout: An even number twice as great as the child's always belongs to the father; the following odd number belongs to the mother. Use the formula, "Number 1 on this chart is the same as number ___ on chart number___ ," to extend a line across multiple charts.

Family Group Charts

Family Group charts (Figure 1-2) enable you to record complete vital data on one couple and their children. For large families and multiple marriages, you simply attach extra sheets to the first.

Family Group charts are designed for compiling data on complete families. Some researchers claim interest only in direct lines (that is, parents, grandparents, great-grandparents, and so forth). However, your ancestors did not live in a vacuum—vital clues about them may not turn up until the entire family (and perhaps even the extended family and neighborhood) has been researched. In most cases, a more encompassing approach results in more productive research.

Family Group Record for Carlton Aaron Pierce   1

Husband: **Carlton Aaron Pierce**
Birth 7 Mar 1851   Peru, Berkshire, MA
Death 31 Oct 1934   Hinsdale, Berkshire, MA
Father: Aaron Peirce   Mother: Martha Thomson

Wife: **Fannie Abigail Francis**
Birth 20 Nov 1857   Windsor, Berkshire, MA
Mar. 29 Oct 1879   Hinsdale, Berkshire, Mass   Carlton Aaron Pierce
Death 22 Mar 1934   Hinsdale, Berkshire, MA
Father: William Porter Francis   Mother: Mary Miranda Spencer

1. **Bessie Francis Pierce**
Birth 19 Sep 1882   Hinsdale, Berkshire, Mass
Mar. 18 Sep 1913   Hinsdale, Berkshire, MA   Nelson Clary EARLE
Death 12 Mar 1958   Pittsfield, Berkshire, MA

2. **Carl Ambrose Pierce**
Birth 26 Jul 1884   Hinsdale, Berkshire, Mass
Mar. 6 Nov 1920   Springfield, Hampden, MA   Emily Wadsworth Robinson
Div.   Jennie Ellis Hutchins
Mar. 9 May 1905   Rockland, MA   Jennie Ellis Hutchins
Death 8 Feb 1945   Pittsfield, Berkshire, MA

3. **Ruth Alida Pierce**
Birth 24 Mar 1894   Hinsdale, Berkshire, MA
Mar. 31 Aug 1915   Hinsdale, Berkshire, Mass   Arthur Percy Chamberlain
Death 8 Jul 1989   Greenwich, Fairfield, CT

Figure 1-2. Family Group Chart

Your research may turn up facts that are beyond the parameters of the fields on the Family Group chart. Record this miscellany in your research log and in a "Notes" field or some other unused space on an appropriate Family Group chart. As later chapters explain, miscellaneous facts may provide crucial clues for further research.

Keeping a Research Log

Record all data, including the records you've searched and the results of searching them, in a research log. Research logs provide a base from which you can pull pieces of data to enter on Family Group charts, Pedigree charts, and other forms. Research logs also provide a paper trail of your research process, which is useful as you analyze data and formulate plans for further research. If you find a piece of data that you know applies to the subject(s) of your research, go ahead and record that data on a Family Group chart, Pedigree chart, or other appropriate form, but be sure to record it in the research log as well.

Generally, you will be more successful in genealogical research if you learn to "survey large fields before cultivating small ones." Therefore, you should record *everything* that you suspect may help you connect family puzzle pieces, not just information for the one person or family you are interested in at the moment. (See Chapter 2 for more information on making and organizing research notes.)

Documenting Sources

As you fill out forms and record research notes, you should habitually and carefully document the source of each piece of data as you obtain it. A simple way to do this is to append superscript numbers (first fact[1], second fact[2], and so on) to each piece of data. Enter the numbers in the "Source of Information" or equivalent field, along with their respective complete source citations, as illustrated in Figure 1-3.

There are compelling reasons for thorough documentation. First, you must know the source of data to evaluate its worth. Second, you may need to recheck this source if you find conflicting data later. And finally, accurate documentation gives credibility to your conclusions, which will enable a third party to use your research.

HUSBAND: James MOORE
Born: 1803[1]   Place: Ireland[1]
Married: Jun 1825[3]   Place: Chester Co., PA[3]
Died: 19 Dec 1888[2]
Buried: Place: Jacksville, Camden Co., IL[2]

WIFE: Ann JONES
Born: 5 Mar 1807[1]   Place: Wales[1]
Father: Evan JONES[1]

CHILDREN	When born	Where born
1. James MOORE	24 Apr 1826[3]	Laurel Hill, Chester Co., PA
2. Ann MOORE	31 May 1829[3]	Laurel Hill, Chester Co., PA

SOURCES OF INFORMATION
[1] Family Bible in possession of Mary Hungate, 246 Main St., Smith City, IA
[2] Tombstone, Jacksville, IL
[3] International Genealogical Index (IGI), 1988 edition

Figure 1-3. Example of Documentation for a Family Group Chart

Because proper documentation helps ensure research quality, genealogy
software that lacks this capability, including the ability to record miscellany,
is unacceptable. Several programs offer automated notation of the type shown
in Figure 1-3.

Obtaining Information From Relatives

Most researchers find that relatives are their best source of data initially.
Learning family history from family members is often both easier and more
interesting than gleaning it from other sources. Relatives can provide anecdotes
and personality, which you seldom find in public records.

Relatives are an especially important source of information for recent
generations. Government and other agencies often refuse to release records
made within the last seventy to one hundred years, since they may contain
information about living persons and, therefore, are considered confidential.
Learn as much as possible from relatives before turning to other resources.
After recording all the facts you know, start contacting relatives, including
distant ones, as you learn about them.

Family reunions provide excellent opportunities to both gather information and
recruit people to help you with family research. At reunions, where many

family members gather in one place, you can quickly determine which relatives are interested in working with you on the family history; genealogical research is easier and more enjoyable when several researchers cooperate. When several family members express interest in their heritage, reunions can become ideal forums for planning, coordinating, and sharing family history research strategies and results.

As you begin gathering information from your relatives, interview older family members first; in addition to having the greatest store of family knowledge, they are likely to die the soonest, taking their storehouse of information to the grave with them. Don't be put off if elderly relatives suffer from senility; your attempts to help them recall early memories will often be rewarding for both you and them.

Interviews

Oral interviewing has recently received the serious attention of scholars and historians. At least two helpful guidelines have emerged from this scrutiny: First, you should show genuine interest in the person you are interviewing, and second, relate your questions to his or her own life. If you want to know the death date of your grandfather's mother, start by asking your grandfather questions about his life. As you both become more comfortable, ask such relevant questions as, "How old were you when your mother died?" or "Where were you living when your mother died?" Tape-record the interview, if possible, but also take notes, particularly of names or places that are unfamiliar to you; ask about these items before finishing the interview. This indirect approach helps to put the interviewee at ease and generally results in a more productive and enjoyable session than does merely requesting facts.

Seldom can you obtain all the information you desire in a single visit. Elderly people often tire after a short time. In addition, memories often surface after you've left and the interviewee continues to ponder your questions. Relatives who haven't talked about their pasts recently may claim not to remember a thing. Don't let such comments deter you. One friend of ours dealt with her grandfather's claim of memory loss by visiting him four times with same set of questions. He recalled more memories each time. Another friend had impatient and uncooperative parents ("I don't remember," or "That's not important"), but made a breakthrough by questioning cooperative in-laws who happened to visit while her parents were present. Influenced by the in-laws' positive attitude, her parents began to volunteer the very facts they had refused to divulge earlier. Often, you can help interviewees feel more comfortable by bringing one of their friends or relatives to the interview to reminisce about "the good old days." If possible, capture these valuable sessions on audio- or video-tape for posterity.

Be sure to ask interviewees about heirlooms, old photos, albums, newspaper clippings, mementos, journals, and letters. These tangible items, as well as oral reminders such as anecdotes or stories, may help jog memories or provide proof or clues regarding dates, places, and relationships. They may also provide fascinating glimpses into the lives, times, and personalities of your ancestors. Using either a still-photo camera or a video camera, you should record this part of the interview as well. (Video camcorders and digital cameras enable you to take still photographs in electronic form. You can view these photos on a computer, then access and edit the images with optical character recognition [OCR] or object linking and embedding [OLE] software.)

Family Myths

If you have played the parlor game Gossip, you know how easy it is for statements to become distorted when passed from person to person. The same process, unfortunately, happens frequently when family members pass historical information from generation to generation. Although orally related information can be valuable, you should be skeptical as you analyze this type of data. (Keep your skepticism to yourself, of course, to avoid offending relatives who put great stock in family myths.)

Be particularly wary of far-fetched or too-good-to-be-true family traditions, such as claims that your ancestry includes royalty, famous historical figures, Mayflower immigrants, and so on. Such stories may tempt you to begin your research with the presumed famous or royal ancestor, but this research strategy is almost always counter-productive. Work from the present back, one generation at a time. Substantiate each link with well-documented evidence, if not legal proof. As your research progresses, you will be able to check out the intriguing possibilities that emerge from family interviews and other sources.

If extensive family research has already been done, "spot-check" the work by looking up a few references. Carefully compare the data in the original records with that extracted from them to evaluate the thoroughness and accuracy of the research.

Computers and Genealogical Research

Increasing numbers of family historians are using computers to organize and store their research. High-quality genealogy software makes it easy to store and retrieve data and to display and print it in useful ways. Fortunately, the price of computers continues to drop even as they become more powerful and easier to use. We advocate the use of computer tools in genealogical research; however, we recognize that purchasing a personal computer may not be possible or even desirable for everyone. Before deciding whether you want to use a computer for your research, you should consider the advantages and disadvantages of this technology.

Advantages

A personal computer can help you organize, record, retrieve, copy, and share your genealogical research.

- **Speed:** A computer can help you search rapidly through lists of names. The speed at which you can conduct a search might range from seconds to minutes, depending on the type of computer you use and the amount of data involved.

- **Accuracy and reproduction:** Good genealogy software packages enable you to enter a piece of information (such as a name and associated family relationships) once, then use that information as often as you desire in a variety of formats; with proper software and a modem, you can even send data, such as family group, pedigree, and ahnentafel charts, electronically to another computer. (An ahnentafel chart [German for "table of ancestors"] is a hierarchical listing of generations.) For example, we use a software application called AskSAM, a database in which we have organized many names and other genealogical information. Often, as we communicate with other computer users, we find people who are researching names that we recognize as being in our database. We use AskSAM to access the information, then edit it in a word processing application, then copy it to another program that enables us to send the information through electronic mail to the person who needs it. The process may sound complicated, but it requires less than five minutes to accomplish because the information is automated and transportable.

- **Compiling information:** Many software applications enable you to sort information such as dates and names. By compiling and viewing this information in different ways, you can often see patterns and relationships, as well as determine what information is missing. For example, we use AskSAM to sort information in a number of ways, including sorting by the name of the first (male) or second (female) godparent for christenings. By finding all the families for which a specific individual acted as a godparent, we discover clues that help us determine how families are linked together.

Disadvantages

Many of the disadvantages associated with computers result from users' ignorance of technology. No matter what its purchase price, a computer is a wise investment only if you are willing to spend time and energy to determine what kind of equipment and software you need, then to learn how to use it once you have made the purchase.

- **Cost:** While the price of computers and their accoutrements continues to fall, a computer is still a major investment, and the more peripheral equipment and software programs you add, the larger that investment becomes. If you have only a vague awareness of your needs, it's easy to overspend by purchasing a more powerful computer or more accessories than you will use. On the other hand, if you're too thrifty, you may end up with a system that isn't powerful enough or doesn't have enough features to be useful. When you decide to buy, talk to people who use computers to perform the same type of tasks for which you will use a computer, read product reviews in computer magazines, and shop around to determine pricing and availability of equipment.

- **Learning curve:** As with any skill, there is the learning curve associated with computer use. Initially you can expect to spend more time mastering new skills than you save on research. Check with universities, community colleges, school districts, and computer stores in your area to see if they offer courses in basic personal computer use and other computer-related skills. Next to hiring a personal tutor, taking one or more of these classes is probably the best way to start the learning process and can help you decide whether you wish to use a computer for your genealogical research.

- **Obsolescence:** The rapidity with which computer hardware becomes obsolete makes it difficult to determine what equipment to buy and when to buy it. However, if you buy wisely, you shouldn't be concerned that the machine you purchase will be obsolete in six months (which is the life-expectancy of today's technology, according to some computer gurus). You can expect several years of good service from your computer—unless technological breakthroughs offer so many practical advantages that you're willing to pay the price for a new machine.

Databases

A database is a more or less structured system for storing information on the computer; the term generally suggests a highly structured electronic software program with automated functions such as searching and retrieval. The electronic database follows the same organizational principles used for the traditional database, which is the file cabinet.

Database software programs tend to be rather rigid in form, composed of fields that are generally of fixed length. Usually, these programs contain several different "screens," which are comparable to paper forms. Each screen contains fields, or areas that correspond to blanks on a paper form. In Figure 1-4, the underlined area to the right of "Last Name" is a field. A field can be indicated on the screen by a blank area next to a word or a phrase, by a distinctive color (if you have a color monitor), or by a blank line. The maximum number of characters that you can enter into a field varies both within and between databases.

```
Last Name: Jackson_____

Birth Date: 08/08/1893

If known, enter the following information:

Birthplace: _____

Mother's Last Name: Anderson_____
```

Figure 1-4. Example of a Screen in a Database

Telecommunications

As increasing numbers of mainstream computer users hop on the information superhighway, online communication is becoming a popular means of getting messages from one point to another. When you use a telephone, you're participating in basic telecommunications. But you can also connect telephone lines to computers so that you can send and receive information through your computer. With a computer, you can communicate with one, several, or hundreds of individuals simultaneously. This makes telecommunications an excellent genealogical resource. The opportunities offered by telecommunications are discussed in more detail in Chapter 11. For now, just be aware that the growing importance of online research makes it an issue you must consider in choosing a computer.

The chapters that follow will provide information about the basics of genealogical research, information resources, and computer technology and its application to your research.

Chapter 2

Organizing Your Research

Whether you are just beginning to uncover your roots or are involved in ongoing genealogical research, organization is essential. If you do not organize your research at the outset, you may soon become overwhelmed by the bits and pieces of information (records, notes, published articles, etc.) that you accumulate. If this happens, it's easy to lose sight of your objectives and become discouraged with the whole endeavor.

Organizing genealogical research involves three basic steps:

- Choosing a family line

- Planning your research

- Keeping and filing notes

Choosing a Family Line

The most important ingredients in successful genealogical research are determination and willingness to learn and adhere to correct research principles. With this attitude, and by tapping recently developed technological resources, you can experience considerable success, even if the ancestral lines in which you are interested are difficult to research.

Of course, you should avoid wasting time and effort on research that has already been done or is being done by someone else. For this reason, you should seek out as many living relatives as possible when you begin research. You should also look for published family histories and check the Ancestral File, which is discussed in Chapter 4.

Personal Interest

Personal interest is the overriding consideration in selecting any family line to research. If you are a beginner, you should generally limit yourself to researching one line at a time. As you talk with relatives, determine which ancestral line really piques your interest. For example, as you interview Aunt Nel about her grandparents, you not only glean data about them, but you also learn of a family Bible they kept, which is now in possession of one of Aunt Nel's cousins. You track down that lead and obtain a photocopy of your great-grandparents' family Bible record. A second cousin tells you about another relative who is researching the family history; you contact him, and he shares the results of his research with you. By making good use of your family network, you may find one or two lines for which you think you can find some important information that will help fit your family puzzle together.

Factors Affecting Ease of Research

Once you have collected and examined all the facts available from family resources, you can expand your research into non-family records. If you're new to genealogical research, you may need to consider the degree of difficulty involved in researching certain lines. Generally, the degree of difficulty in research depends upon several characteristics of the ancestral line: the language in which records are written; the location and availability of records; and the geographical stability and social status of the family.

Language
Unless you have the help of a translator, you'll find it difficult to gather information from documents recorded in a language you can't read. The word lists available at the family history centers operated by The Church of Jesus Christ of Latter-day Saints (the LDS church) or at the LDS Family History Library in Salt Lake City, Utah can help you get started.

Location of Records
Generally, the repositories that contain records about your ancestors will be located in or near the area where they lived. If that area is far from your residence, you may find that research is frustrating and obtaining records you need is expensive. For this reason, you should consider beginning your research with families who resided closest to your home. However, if you enjoy and can afford intercontinental travel, or if a nearby genealogical collection contains many of the records you need, your research can still be successful. Otherwise, consider researching those families who resided closest to where you live.

Telecommunications advances are beginning to reduce the problem of accessing remote information. If your research requires international communication, consider making online connections through the Internet and other sources. See Chapter 11 for more information about these growing possibilities.

Availability of Records
After you've learned which repositories *may* contain records for your ancestors, your next task is determining whether the records actually exist. Obviously, the more records you can find for a family, the easier your research

will be. If you find a dearth of records for one line, you may wish to choose another line and postpone researching the first line until you have more experience or until additional resources become available.

Examples of difficult areas to research are parts of tidewater and eastern Virginia, which are considered "burned-out" sections for genealogists. During the Civil War, county clerks throughout that region were ordered to send their counties' parish records to Richmond for safe keeping. Unfortunately, Richmond was razed by the Union army, and most of the records were destroyed. Many other Southern cities were also left in ruins; generally, the farther south your ancestors lived, the more difficult it will be to locate their records. However, some excellent resources are being compiled and published for the South, so research in that area becomes easier each year.

Because Northern cities fared much better in the Civil War, early New England records (both civil and church) are more complete than Southern records. Thus, if you are a beginner, you should consider tracing a pre-Civil War New England line before a Southern line of the same period. Similarly, consider tracing English lines before Irish lines—many Irish records were lost when the national record office was destroyed in 1921.

In addition to large-scale destruction from wars, small-scale disasters have also caused records to be lost. For example, many individual churches, court houses, and other record repositories have flooded or burned. Some county clerks and ministers were careless or lacked space to keep the records at the courthouse or church. Some of these records ended up in attics, cubbyholes, or even garbage cans. Others—as we witness occasionally—are eventually rediscovered and made available.

You can consult two main resources to learn which records have survived and are available: The LDS Family History Library and historical societies. The LDS Family History Department generally does not microfilm records housed by local historical societies, so you'll find few duplicate records as you check out these two resources.

- **LDS Family History Library:** The *Family History Library Catalog* is published by the LDS Family History Library in Salt Lake City, Utah. For each area of the world, the catalog lists specific records that are on microfilm and available for research. The microfilming of records is an ongoing effort, and the catalog is updated regularly. You can obtain the records through any LDS family history center. See Chapter 4 for more information on both the LDS Family History Library and local family history centers.

- **Historical societies:** Historical societies located in the areas in which your ancestors lived can be another fruitful resource. These societies employ experts who can answer your questions concerning record sources and accessibility. Chapter 5 provides details for using these societies.

Geographical Stability

A family that remained in the same town for generations will be easier to research than one that moved often across county or state lines. Cross-country migration was common during the early history of the United States, especially in the era following the Revolutionary War. The decades from 1790 to 1850 have been labelled the "black-out" period, partly because of mass migration, and also because pre-1850 census records provide such scanty family information. In general, these decades in American history are the most difficult to research for ancestral records.

However, many helpful resources are emerging to improve this situation. A number of census indexes have been published since the U.S. Bicentennial, and many Revolutionary War pension applications are also being indexed and published. In many instances, you can use these records to trace families two to three generations following the Revolutionary War.

Social Issues

Historically, a family's place in society has affected the quality and volume of records that were kept for family members. Two factors seem especially relevant: The family's socioeconomic status, and the responsibility family members felt to keep their name "respectable."

- **Status:** Families with relatively high social status tend to be easier to research than others. The more prominent a family, the more records (including wills and land records) they are likely to have left. Literacy was usually limited to society's upper classes, and property holders usually kept track of their ancestry for purposes of inheritance. Normally, the earlier the era, the greater the importance of social prominence becomes if you hope to find family records. By the Middle Ages in Europe, only nobility and royal lines can be researched with much success.

- **Family skeletons:** Family skeletons, or unsavory family secrets, make some lines difficult to research. Most of us would not be upset to discover among our ancestors a grandfather who was a horse thief, or a grandmother who ran off with a scalawag; in fact, such discoveries would probably excite us. But our ancestors may have been less accepting. You may need sleuthing skills to uncover certain facts, if family members wanted to keep them buried.

Planning Your Research: Goals and Biographies

After choosing a line to research, you must formulate a research plan. Begin your plan by writing down the specific facts you want to find; that is, state your goals—what are you trying to accomplish through your research? Next, write a biography of each person whose history you wish to research. (See the section later in this chapter titled "Writing Goals and Biographies: A Scenario" for an example of setting goals and writing biographies.) Include as much of the following information as you know:

• Approximate or known ages

• Places and dates of residence

• Social status (Note amount of property owned from land or census records and titles of respect)

• Ethnic and religious background

• Names of children, spouse(s), siblings, parents, and any other known or suspected relatives

Revisit these biographies regularly, re-analyzing and revising as needed. As you gain experience in genealogical analysis, you will be able to use these facts to plan and implement productive research.

A computer is especially useful for recording facts and creating biographies. Using a word processing program, you can type notes and file them electronically. You can then organize your files logically so that you can retrieve your notes quickly and easily, rather than spend time rummaging through boxes or stacks of file folders.

Facts Required

A sound research strategy begins with facts you already have. Specifically, to research a family you must have the following information:

• Names

• Places, or geography (Last known location—if you don't yet know your ancestors' specific locale, use indexes or other finding aids to obtain this information)

• Dates, or history (Time period during which the family resided at that location)

Perhaps the family records you have collected and organized contain these facts. However, you may have only names. If this is the case, you must look for clues to help you establish dates and locations.

Our experience is that analytical skills are the most important element distinguishing successful researchers from unsuccessful ones. If you know very few facts when you begin, analyze what little you have, act on your conclusions, then repeat the whole process. You'll soon outdistance those who start with a lot of data but don't know what to make of it.

The information that follows will help you find the names, locations, and time periods you must know before you can conduct more in-depth research.

Names

Many factors regarding both given names and surnames can help or hinder your search for an ancestor's identity. The discussions below provide valuable hints on finding the names you need for your family tree.

Common Names

Having to deal with a very common surname can hamper your search, not only because you must record every entry for that surname in each record you search, but also because the likelihood of mistaking identity increases.

Families with common surnames may be especially difficult to research if they used common first names as well. Fortunately, some families with common surnames have made themselves more identifiable by using distinctive first, or Christian, names. These names, as we'll discuss later, were usually passed on through successive generations; just one or two of these names can make quite a difference in helping you distinguish your particular Brown, Davis, or Sullivan family from others.

Surname Origins

In general, modern surnames originated from one of the following sources:

• Rank or occupation (For example, Cooper, Smith, Davin [Irish for *poet*], Major)

• Location (For example, Hill, Washington, Holland)

• Animal, vegetable, or mineral (For example, Fox, Chestnut, Silver)

• Personal names (For example, Abraham, Dobkins [affectionate form of "Little Rob"].) This category includes patronymic names, meaning names formed from the given name of a child's father with the addition of a prefix or suffix. See examples in Table 2-1.

Table 2-1. Examples of Patronymic Names

Surnames	Meaning	Nationality
McDonald/MacDonald	Son or descendant of Donald	Scotch
O'Conner	Son or descendant of Conner	Irish
Price (originally: Ap Rice)	Son or descendant of Rice	Welsh
Evans	Son or descendant of Evan	Welsh
Johnson/Jones	Son or descendant of John	English/Welsh
Rasmussen	Son or descendant of Rasmus	Scandinavian
Andreiovich	Son or descendant of Andrei	Russian

At various times in our history, ethnic groups have tended to follow certain occupations, resulting in such stereotypes as the Irish policeman. Knowing your ancestors' work histories, along with the original surname form, may help you determine their ethnic backgrounds. See Sowell's *Immigrant America* for more information.

If the family you are researching bears a rare or local surname, a good index, such as the International Genealogical Index (IGI), published by the Family History Department of The Church of Jesus Christ of Latter-day Saints, may lead you to the place from which the family came. For example, if all entries for a maternal surname occur in only one town in Germany, and entries for the paternal surname are also found there, this is quite possibly the ancestral town. Such evidence is most convincing, of course, in countries for which the index includes much of the early population and in which many surnames are local (that is, found in only one part of that country). Local surnames are quite common, for example, in Italy and the Germanic countries.

Christian Names and Naming Patterns

The names of saints were adopted as first names during the Christianization of Europe. However, naming practices developed differently in different countries. For example, Catholic families in Germany and France generally gave at least two baptismal names to each child. The first name was usually the same for all children of the same gender within a family, so each child went by the second (or last, if there were more than two) given name.

Certain given names were more common in specific countries, as children were often named after popular kings, queens, or (often religious) heroes and heroines. Mary (or Maria), for example, was the most popular female name in many Catholic countries.

Given names are important to genealogical research because families generally used the same names through successive generations. A study comparing historical child-naming practices in a German town and a Massachusetts town found that naming the eldest son after the father, and the eldest daughter after the mother, was equally common in both cultures in the late seventeenth century, with the practice gradually declining in later generations.

Analyzing the names and naming practices used by a family around the time of immigration can help you determine the family's country of origin. Recurrence of the Christian name Cornelius, for example, might indicate either Dutch or Irish origins, since it was a popular name with both those ethnic groups. If you also find Patrick, Dennis, and Bridget in the same line, Irish descent is a strong possibility; however, names such as Jan, Hendrick (Henry), and Gertrude would indicate likely Dutch origins.

Many Scottish families used the following naming pattern: The oldest son was named after the paternal grandfather, the second son after the maternal grandfather, the eldest daughter after the maternal grandmother, and the second daughter after the paternal grandmother. This pattern was also commonly used in many of the British Isles, including Ireland, and the pattern often extended even further: The third son was named after the father, the fourth son after the father's oldest brother, the fifth son after the mother's oldest brother, the third daughter after the mother, the fourth daughter after the mother's oldest sister, the fifth daughter after the father's oldest sister, and so on.

The most common Dutch naming pattern was similar: The first son was named for his paternal grandfather, the second son for his maternal grandfather, the third son for his father's paternal grandfather, the fourth son for his mother's paternal grandfather, the fifth son for his father's maternal grandfather, and the sixth son for his mother's maternal grandfather. The first daughter was named for her maternal grandmother, the second for her paternal grandmother, the third for her mother's maternal grandmother, the fourth for her father's maternal grandmother, the fifth for her mother's paternal grandmother, and the sixth for her father's paternal grandmother.

Rigid naming patterns were often followed closely in the "old country," but usually these traditions were discontinued as immigrants assimilated into the

U.S. melting pot. Moreover, the patterns were often interrupted if a parent or sibling died. In this case, the next child was often named for the deceased parent or sibling.

We have noticed a fairly common naming pattern associated with re-marriage from the seventeenth and even up to, and as late as, the nineteenth century in this country. In this pattern, when people remarried following the death of a spouse, the new couple's first child of the same gender as the deceased spouse was named after the deceased. In some cases, the deceased spouse's surname, rather than the first name, became the child's given name.

In New England it was common for the son who bore his father's name to have the exclusive right of passing that name on to one of his sons. His brothers generally did not give that name to any of their sons. In the Southern states, on the other hand, it was common for male cousins in each branch of the family to bear their paternal grandfather's given name.

The practice of giving two living children in the same family identical given names (usually the same as the parent) was common in England during medieval times but disappeared by about the mid-1600s. Therefore, finding two siblings with the same name in a later time period generally indicates that the elder of the two died (or was expected to die) prior to the baptism or naming of the second.

Using Names and Other Evidence for Identification
Names alone are generally not adequate proof of descent, as you'll quickly realize if you attempt to trace the ancestry of a William Smith or Mary Jones. It would be naive to assume that a John Nott born in one place is the same person as, or even related to, a John Nott whose marriage record is found in another place a generation or so later. A name is circumstantial evidence only; seek other evidence to confirm or disprove identity.

Be prepared for some confusion; we have observed that variants were used almost interchangeably for some names well into the nineteenth century. For example, the name Nuckols includes, among its variety of spellings, the common Nichols and Nicholas. Thus, records containing the name John Nicholas might refer to your ancestor John Nuckols or to a completely unrelated person. By considering such possibilities, you can begin your search for additional evidence to determine identity. (Other examples of commonly interchanged names include Williams and Williamson; Robinson, Robison, Robertson, Robins and Roberts; Davis, Daves, Davies, and David; and Dixon, Dickeson, Dickenson, Dickerson, Dickson, and Dix.)

Nicknames

Nicknames were common and helpful in establishing identities in places with a limited supply of traditional Christian-and-surname combinations. For instance, if ten contemporaries named John Sullivan lived in a small Irish town, each might bear a descriptive nickname such as One-Eyed John, Red John, Long John, and so on.

Standard nicknames were even more commonly used. Table 2-2 lists popular female nicknames.

Table 2-2. Popular Female Nicknames

Given Name	Common Nickname(s)
Abigail	Abby, Gail, Nabby
Agnes	Annis, Aggie, Nessie
Ann	Nancy, Nannie
Dorothy	Dolly, Dottie
Ellen, Helen, Eleanor, Eleanora, Ellie, Nellie	(Given names used interchangeably as nicknames)
Elizabeth	Eliza, Liz, Lizzie, Bess, Betsy
Euphan	Fanny, Phaney
Frances	Fanny, Frankey
Jean, Janet, Joan, Jennie	(Given names used interchangeably as nicknames)
Johannah, Anna, Hannah	(Given names used interchangeably as nicknames)
Lettice, Letitia	Liddy
Matilda	Matty, Til
Mary	Polly, Molly, May
Martha	Patsey, Patty, Matty
Margaret	Peggy, Maggie, Meg

Given Name	Common Nickname(s)
Sarah	Sally, Sadie
Susan	Sukey, Susie

As you can see, standard nicknames aren't always obvious. This may cause problems, especially if a family was inconsistent in how they referred to a child, or if an individual began using a different version of the name upon reaching adulthood. Another situation that may cause you grief is a family's giving similar names to two or more children. One family we researched included a daughter named Anna by a first wife and another named Anne by a second wife. Until we realized this, we made all kinds of mistakes by confusing the two girls as one. Steward's *American Given Names* and Hanks and Hodges' *A Dictionary of Surnames* are helpful references for tracking down nicknames.

Descriptive Tags
Other means of identification, such as occupation, age, family relationships, military rank, residence, personal description, ethnic group, or social class were often appended to names in documents. Land deeds and court documents, for example, often contained descriptive "tags" to help distinguish same-named neighbors. The examples in Table 2-3, drawn from colonial America, are typical.

Signatures, Marks, Slave Names, Coats-of-Arms
Because each person's signature is unique, you can sometimes use signatures to determine whether a signed record pertains to your ancestor or to some other person with the same name. Be sure to examine adjacent records, however, because if the handwriting looks the same in each signature, they were doubtless all signed by the county clerk.

Illiterate individuals used a mark rather than a signature. However, a literate person who was very feeble (as in the case of a deathbed will) might also have used a mark. If your ancestor's mark was the common "X," it won't help you to prove identity. But people with common names often adopted unique marks, and county clerks and record-abstractors often copied them accurately enough to make positive identification possible even if you're using copied or published sources.

Slave names, recorded in tax, deed, will, or other records, provide circumstantial evidence of descent and relationships for black pedigrees, as well as for white slaveholding families.

Coats-of-arms may not only provide the link between an immigrant and a foreign ancestor, but can also be used to distinguish between individuals of the same surname wherever they appear. Woodcock and Robinson's *The Oxford Guide to Heraldry* can help you trace your ancestry using coats-of-arms. Livestock brands recorded in county records provide yet another means of identification.

Table 2-3. Descriptive Tags from Colonial America

Name	Tag	Identifier
Mary Smith	daughter of William	Family
David Miller	Tom's Creek or T.C.	Residence (often abbreviated)
James Jones	"redhead"	Description or nickname
John Paul	carpenter	Occupation (Note: Occasionally an indexer may mistakenly include occupation as part of the name; "John Paul Carpenter" might be the wrongly indexed entry in this case.)
Thomas Howard	Capt.	Military title (Note: This title may also refer to the occupation of ship captain.)
William Mosely	Dutchman	Ethnic group (Note: "Deutsche," or German, heritage was sometimes written incorrectly as "Dutch;" in this case, you should check other sources to determine ethnicity.)
Michael King	Gent.	Abbreviation for gentleman
Bruce Guernsey	Jr.	Age
James Bradley	dec'd	Abbreviation for deceased

Surnames Used as Christian Names

In England and the American colonies—especially in the South—it became common some centuries ago to use a mother's maiden surname as a son's first name (or, occasionally, a daughter's). Thus, John Smith and Mary Miles might name a son Miles Smith. When Miles Smith married Ann, daughter of Edwin Dixon, their sons' names might include Dixon, Miles, John, Edwin, and/or Edwin Dixon.

In about the mid-eighteenth century, middle names became more common than they had been. Both sons and daughters were commonly given their fathers' or grandfathers' given names, family surnames, or other relatives' names as their first or middle names. Names could be long: Hunter Graham Ingram Archer Jones and Maria Randolph Carter Ambler Ruffin are two examples. Generally, each name signified part of the family tree (though not always in a direct line). One common practice, for instance, was naming a child after a deceased sibling—either the child's or a parent's—especially if that sibling had lived to be a married adult but died without issue. It was also common to name a younger child for a distant relative, especially one with social prominence. We found one youngest child named after his step-grandmother's first husband! The relationship is usually much closer. If your ancestors followed such naming practices, you can gain helpful clues by learning the complete names of all family members.

Initials were often used in place of especially long names, such as J.H.W.R. Jones, especially among the English. You may need to consult family Bibles and birth or christening records to discover the names to which these initials refer. Occasionally, you'll find a disappointing case in which initials refer to nothing more than initials!

Popular and romanticized given names have become common in modern times, as the centuries-old practice of using traditional family names has gradually been discarded. Thus, beginning in about the mid-nineteenth century, first names are less useful for identifying family lines. Before that time, the common use of surnames as given names in some areas, and the use of traditional names passed on for several generations in most areas, provide clues that may help you discover maternal lines.

Naming patterns can be quite complex, however. Related families often intermarried, and hero names occasionally supplanted family names. Popular names of the Revolutionary War era include George Washington, Patrick Henry, and forms of Marquis Lafayette, such as Fayette and Mark. Occasionally the hero might be a locally popular minister, a midwife, a business partner, or a family friend. If you've hypothesized that your ancestors' Christian names indicate an earlier family surname, be sure to substantiate this hypothesis with adequate research.

Maiden Names and the Rights of Married Women

The status of women in different countries, states, and eras affects genealogical research. The earlier the date in most English-speaking, non-Catholic countries, the fewer maiden names are written in records. In one set of marriage records that we checked for Augusta County (the parent county of western Virginia and many points westward), only the names of the grooms were recorded, presumably to save record space—and this was as late as the 1760s! During this same period, on the other hand, an Episcopal minister in a nearby part of Virginia included mothers' maiden names in their children's christening records. Both recording practices were unusual for this state and time.

Under common law, a married woman was not allowed to make a will, sell land, or otherwise direct the disposition of her property. This was often true even when a marriage settlement, or prenuptial agreement, stipulated otherwise. Obviously, this affected record-keeping practices. Generally, you'll not find land or will records for a married woman until and unless she was widowed, if she lived in a state operating under English common law. However, several states (Arizona, California, Idaho, Louisiana, New Mexico, Nevada, Texas, and Washington) employed the Spanish, or community, property law; in these states, you may find records filed under a wife's name.

Places (Geography)

Obviously, your ancestors' geographical locations influenced their lives. Taking some time to understand that influence will help to advance your research. Using genealogical indexes such as the IGI, you may be able to determine the county or parish in which your ancestor lived. Census indexes can also help you to determine ancestors' places of residence. Many other indexes are also available, and a number more are being compiled. You should consult updated guidebooks to learn what indexes exist for your area of interest. We've listed several of these guidebooks in the bibliography at the end of this chapter.

Obtaining Quality Maps and Atlases

You should examine maps early in your research project. Study and make photocopies of appropriate maps, especially those contemporary with the time period of your research. You can usually find the maps you need at a major research library in or near the location you are researching. Local genealogical and historical societies may also have helpful maps. Often, these organizations can also direct you to suppliers or repositories.

Gazetteers and other references may include genealogical data with their geographical information. For example, while researching early New York, we found an 1860 gazetteer that provided historical and geographical data, along with the names of the earliest settlers of the area. In one case, the gazetteer even named the Connecticut town from which these settlers emigrated, which helped us immensely with our research. (Another source of genealogical data is early land-ownership maps, which often include landowners' names.)

Finding Residence

You'll be able to find records of your ancestors much more quickly if you know where they lived. Generally, you need to know the **county** for states in the U.S., and the county (or equivalent jurisdiction) as well as **town** or **parish** for Europe and the New England states. Say your ancestors came from Hard Rock, Kansas; in order to find the county in which Hard Rock is located, you must either locate the town on a Kansas map or look it up in a gazetteer, the *Family History Library Catalog,* or some other reference.

If family records name an immigrant's birthplace as Eastersnow, Ireland, first you must determine whether that place was a parish, town or townland, province, barony, diocese, or county. Then you must find Eastersnow's location in Ireland. If boundaries and place names have remained relatively stable, a current map will suffice for such research. If not, you should consult older maps, postal guides, shipping almanacs, or gazetteers.

Because some immigrants earned passage money in a port city prior to departure, families may have mistakenly named that city as the birthplace. If family lore claims family origin at major ports such as Liverpool, Cork, or Hamburg, you should find corroborating documentation.

If you are still unsuccessful, examine even earlier maps and historical gazetteers; perhaps the location no longer exists under the name you are looking for. Two good references are Parker's *Library Service for Genealogists* (quite good for the U.S., and conveniently lists sources by individual state), and Abate's *Omni Gazetteer of the United States* (also available in a CD-ROM version).

Our experience in tracing a Scottish line helps illustrate the important relationship between geographical and genealogical facts. Several years ago, we traced this line by first examining family data; we learned that our immigrant ancestor once wrote his birthplace as Kinner and once as Larbor, while his wife consistently gave hers as Alloa. We then began our geographical search in a nearby university library that housed a good worldwide map and gazetteer collection. In Lewis' excellent *Topographical Dictionary for Scotland,* we found listings for the small mining town, Kinnaird, located in Larbert Parish, Sterlingshire, adjacent to tiny Clackmannanshire, Scotland, where we found the town of Alloa.

Having located their precise birthplaces, we then searched through the excellent Scottish collection in the LDS Family History Library. By examining microfilmed census and parish records, we were able to add several generations of Scottish forebears to our pedigree. We could not have done any of this, of course, without first determining the exact location of our ancestors' birth.

Boundary Changes

Political boundary changes can complicate your search for your ancestors' records. The U.S., a relatively new and fast-growing country, has experienced numerous boundary changes. As one extreme example, we found pertinent sources for an area in present-day Delaware among colonial Pennsylvania, Maryland, and even New York records! If your ancestors lived in any area that experienced numerous boundary or name changes, you may need to consult old maps to find exact place names and/or the correct geographical jurisdictions for your research.

Records from the original county were usually preserved when an offshoot county was formed. One of our ancestors lived long enough to leave records in four different counties, even though he never left the ancestral homestead. The following reference books can help you trace past U.S. boundary changes: Thorndale and Dollarhide's *Map Guide to the U.S. Federal Censuses 1790-1920, Ancestry's Red Book,* and Long's *Atlas of Historical County Boundaries* (a series). A variety of software programs can also help you.

Much of Europe, including the old Austro-Hungarian and German Empires, and the more recent Soviet bloc, have experienced dramatic boundary shifts. But you'll encounter boundary changes even in areas with relatively stable histories. In England, for instance, several counties were divided or renamed in 1974. When you trace boundary changes, pay attention to specific dates and areas involved. Genealogy Unlimited, Inc. (800-666-4363) claims it can locate "most towns in 1871-1918 German Empire." Jonathan Sheppard Books also locates hard-to-find place names using its extensive collection of more than two hundred worldwide maps.

Internet users enjoy an advantage in researching boundary changes. For example, after spending years trying to locate a small German town, one user requested information through the soc.culture.german newsgroup. Within twenty-four hours, six people (five of whom lived in Germany) informed this user of the town's location. (See Chapter 11 for more information on the Internet.)

Topography

Let's say you learn that your ancestor Cyrus Brown lived in Hard Rock, Kansas. You learn that Hard Rock was in Sassafras County when the Cyrus Brown family lived there, so you expect to find the family's vital records in that county seat. By checking a topographical map, however, you find that a rugged, hilly area separates Hard Rock from the county seat. Furthermore, Hard Rock is on the perimeter of the county and is closer to an adjacent county seat than to its own. If a search of the Sassafras County records yields no relevant data, you should check the records of the adjacent county.

Because a topographical map shows the physical characteristics of the land, it can help you spot such boundary problems. A topographical map of a large area can also help you determine probable migration routes used by your ancestors, since such routes developed in accordance with natural surroundings, generally following the path of least resistance.

Dates (History)

In addition to learning about geography, you should read local and regional histories of the area in which your ancestors lived. You can find relevant historical works by using library catalogs, including the Locality section of the *Family History Library Catalog,* as well as bibliographies. As you become familiar with the history of an area, you will probably notice that isolated facts begin to make sense or "fit," just as studying a picture of a completed jigsaw puzzle helps you fit the individual pieces together.

Once you are familiar with the geography and history, you need to learn about sources and records, including their availability, their location, and their purpose. Based on this information, you can complete an effective and realistic research plan. You can find numerous books, pamphlets, and guides on methods of researching particular countries, regions, states, and counties. If possible, start with the Research Outlines available at the LDS Family History Library and family history centers. They are current, inexpensive, and brief, yet quite thorough. If you are connected to the Internet, you can download this information free of charge (see Chapter 11).

U.S. researchers should also use *Ancestry's Red Book* and *The Source,* two comprehensive guidebooks listed in the bibliography at the end of this chapter. Local historical or genealogical societies can supply you with good suggestions as well.

Jurisdictions

Your ancestors may have been involved in a myriad of organizations, or jurisdictions. As residents or citizens of a country, your ancestors' lives were tracked by at least one jurisdiction: The government. Government records include censuses, probates, naturalizations, and land sales. Your ancestors' families comprise another jurisdiction; the family may have kept records of birth dates, baptisms, marriages, and other information. Other organizations that kept records for their members include churches, schools, fraternities, businesses, hospitals, and prisons.

Which records to search

Because direct, primary evidence is best (see Chapter 3), you should begin your search by examining the jurisdictions that produce vital records. The last section of this book provides instructions for finding and using these records. You may find that a thorough search of the record groups discussed will enable you to find the data you need.

Usually, family and government records provide the best information. However, if the records from these jurisdictions are inadequate, you'll need to consider additional jurisdictions. Records from these other organizations can be very helpful. For example, our lineage includes some Irish-Canadian and Irish-Pennsylvanian families with common Irish surnames such as Sullivan, Daugherty, and McCormick. Few family facts had been passed down through these lines, and, because most family members were illiterate and poor, they left few land and probate records. Moreover, Canadians are difficult to locate in census records as few have been indexed. These families would have been poor researching prospects indeed, were it not for one important advantage: They were Catholic.

The Catholic church generally kept thorough, accurate records. Even marginally active members used the local priests to perform marriages and christen children, so parish records are fairly complete. Christening records often include the mother's maiden name, and occasionally priests added other enlightening facts, such as the parents' names of the individuals who served as godparents, or the bride and groom's birth places.

In addition, the church helps researchers: The Catholic priests to whom we have written have generally responded with helpful information. (When requesting such help, we include a small donation in appreciation of the effort required to find, copy, and send two or three complete record entries.) See also Virginia Humling's *U.S. Catholic Sources: A Diocesan Research Guide,* published in 1995 by Ancestry Incorporated.

Necessary background

Our knowledge of our ancestors' Catholicism did not help our research until we learned *what kind* of Catholic records existed, *where* they were, and *how* to obtain them. Fortunately, this information is quite simple to obtain once the records either have been published or have been microfilmed by the LDS church; and many records have been through one of these processes. Chapter 4 of this book explains how you can use the *Family History Library Catalog* and the IGI, both published by the LDS church, to ascertain the extent of published materials, microfilming, and record extraction for any given locality.

If microfilming is incomplete and nothing has been published for the records you need, you will need to consult other resources to obtain the "what," "where," and "how" information. Guidebooks and other research aids for the area you are researching can help you determine which records exist, their location, and methods of obtaining them. Occasionally, you may need to consult with an expert to get the information you need. Genealogical and historical societies can recommend people who can help you; you may also find experts through your telecommunications searches.

For our Sullivan, Daugherty, and McCormick lines, many of the Catholic church records have been published or microfilmed recently. In addition, some helpful Canadian land and vital records have been computerized and published by the Canadian government. We have ordered some of these records through our local LDS family history center. We are also downloading sections of the 1871 Ontario census index from the Freenet (see Chapter 11) in Ottawa (telnet freenet.carleton.ca). These developments are greatly facilitating our research of our Irish-Canadian ancestors. Because so much genealogical information has been microfilmed or otherwise published—and automated in many cases—tracking down important research material is becoming easier.

Age and Legality in the American Colonies
To help those trying to find dates for ancestors who lived during the American colonial era, we've compiled some information regarding age requirements for engaging in certain legal procedures. The English common law system, which was followed in all of the thirteen colonies (except those settled by the Spanish or French), stipulated that a person must meet one of two age requirements to engage in legal actions: First, the age of discretion (legally, a person under this age was known as a "child of tender years"); second, legal age, or adulthood ("minor" or "infant of tender years" were legal terms for a person under this age). These two ages were, respectively, twelve and eighteen for females; fourteen and twenty-one for males.

For instance, a male who was orphaned at age thirteen would be subject to a court-appointed guardian, but at fourteen he could choose his own guardian. If you find among county records a dated entry for your great-grandaunt requesting her eldest brother (your great-grandfather) to be her guardian, you can approximate both their ages. On this date she was between twelve and eighteen years old, while he was at least twenty-one, the minimum age requirement for a guardian. If you find a guardian record dated June 1797 for an under-age male ancestor, and then find him on a jury, acting as a plaintiff in a trial, or writing a will bequeathing land during the month of March 1798, you can assume (as such activities could be initiated only by one of legal age) a birth date between June 1776 and March 1777.

The earliest guardian record for a minor or child makes it possible to approximate a parent's otherwise unknown death date. Parental consent on a marriage record also helps approximate ages; in most states, a minor could not marry without the written consent of a parent or guardian. All states required the bride and groom to have attained at least the age of discretion; some required an additional two or three years.

Because the age at which males could be taxed varied between sixteen and twenty-one, you may need to learn specific information from tax legislation for the appropriate state. In Virginia, for instance, many county tithable (tax) exist, providing a valuable research source for the eighteenth century. The taxpayer was listed first, followed by the names or numbers of the male members of his family over sixteen years of age, then overseers or bound servants, and finally male and female slaves over age sixteen. The Revolutionary War brought some changes to Virginia's tax system: From October 1777 to May 1783, the age requirement for charging sons as tithables was raised to twenty-one. After May 1783, legislation gave county courts authority to list free male tithables aged sixteen through twenty-one. Knowing this information has enabled us to use tithable lists to deduce ages more accurately for young men of this time.

Writing Goals and Biographies: A Scenario

Suppose you want to know the birth dates, birthplaces, and parents of your ancestors Cyrus Brown and Mary Funk. These are your goals. By writing them down and referring to them often, you won't be drawn into unproductive tangents, and you'll be able to record your progress.

Once you have accumulated and organized some information about early family members, write a brief biography of each one. Leave room to add questions or possible sources that may come to mind as you review these facts. The following hypothetical example includes information gathered from family interviews, with analysis and procedures:

Cyrus Brown was a farmer whose earliest known residence (circa 1885) was Hard Rock, Kansas. By checking a map or gazetteer, you learn that Hard Rock is located in Rye County. Because Cyrus was a farmer, there may be Hard Rock land records for him; his earliest deed may even provide his prior residence. You should check the Rye County courthouse for these records, as well as any birth or marriage records for the family.

Cyrus was married to Mary Funk. Her mother's maiden name was Ethel Showalter. Cyrus and Mary are known to have had four children: Mary, Ellen, Barbara, and George. Barbara married Bill Read in Hard Rock. George married Anne; her surname and their marriage place are unknown. As you search the county records, you should look for Funks, Showalters, and Reads, as well as Browns.

While doing some research at a library, you find a deed for Cyrus Brown's purchase of 200 acres of land in Hard Rock, Kansas, in 1887. Because you are interested in Cyrus' birth date, your first impression may be that this document is irrelevant and doesn't need to be recorded. However, our experience is that most records involving our ancestors provide useful facts or clues. For instance, the date of the land purchase helps you deduce that Cyrus was born before 1866, because he had to be at least twenty-one years old to make such a transaction. Therefore, the deed does help you achieve your objective. If the deed names others, such as those *from* whom or *with* whom he purchased the land, you may find other clues for your research.

By 1898, Cyrus had died and the family had moved to Colorado. There may an obituary and probate records for Cyrus in Hard Rock, Kansas; you should check for them at the county courthouse. (Also, check the 1900 Colorado census index and census to pick up the ages of remaining family members and to learn the state of birth for Mary Funk.)

Mary Funk Brown was remarried at an unknown date to one James Brown; they had no children. Could James be related to Cyrus? Maybe you will find information about him as you gather Brown data from the Rye County courthouse. You will want to look for this family under the names of both James Brown and Mary Brown on the 1900 Colorado census, as you don't yet know if they were married by this date.

You will also look for Cyrus and Mary's daughter Barbara under the name of her husband, William or Bill Read, on both the Kansas and Colorado census indexes. Because she married in Hard Rock, the marriage probably—though not necessarily—occurred before the family left there in 1898; check the Rye County marriage records. The 1900 census should list Barbara's birth date and birthplace, providing Cyrus and Mary's probable residence at the time Barbara was born. You should then try to locate the family on earlier censuses. Unfortunately, most of the 1890 census was destroyed in a fire, so try the 1880 Soundex. (For more information about the Soundex, see Chapter 7 and Appendix A.) If you do find Cyrus on the 1880 census or Mary on either the 1880 or 1900 census, you will have not only the place and approximate date of birth for both names, but also the states of birth reported for their parents.

You can use the 1920 census Soundex index to find additional information on James and Mary, if either of them lived that long. The 1910 Colorado census would also be worth searching, but as no index for it exists currently, you could find them easily only if they lived in the same place as they did in 1900 or 1920 (other census years). Therefore, you should note their exact township and street name when you find them on the 1900 census, and if you find them on the 1920 census.

If James or Mary was still living in 1910, that year's census will show the number of years they had been married and the number of previous marriages for each. Knowing the marriage year will help you find their marriage certificate, which may supply facts about Mary Funk's origin and perhaps, indirectly, something about Cyrus' origin, if he was related to James. If the census shows, for instance, that James was Mary's third husband, you would suspect that she had been married once before she was married to Cyrus and that Funk might have been a married name, rather than her maiden name. If you can't find the marriage record for Mary and Cyrus, perhaps your search for the record of her earlier marriage will yield her maiden name.

The Browns were known to be Lutherans, which is helpful; you can write to the Hard Rock Lutheran Church to ask what church records exist for that time period and how you may use them. Or, you can look up that denomination in *The Source,* which informs you that ninety-five percent of American Lutheran Churches are listed by synod in the *Lutheran Church Directory for the United States* (New York: Lutheran Council in the USA, 1976), that extensive microfilming of these records has begun, and that a microfiche catalog of those microfilmed records is available. Because Lutheran church records are among the best genealogically, you definitely want to track down these records.

Learning Specific Places and Times: A Scenario

Suppose all you initially know about an ancestor is his name, Newel Adams, and that he served four years as a Confederate soldier in the U.S. Civil War. You can assume that he lived in a Southern state and that he was at least fourteen years old when he enlisted. By subtracting fourteen from 1860, you conclude that he was born no later than 1846.

However, while interviewing relatives you learn that Newel's youngest son, your great-grandfather, was born in 1871. Newel's eldest grandchild was also born that year. These facts allow you to move Newel's probable birth date back more than a decade. If he had a grandchild born in 1871, Newel was probably born no later than 1837. (We deduce this by twice subtracting a minimum marriage age of seventeen from 1871.)

You also learn that Newel's family was thought to have lived in Kentucky. The 1880 census index that covers families with children ten years of age or under should include this family. If they were in Kentucky in 1880, you can locate them through a Soundex search of that index. The 1880 census contains names, ages, relationships to head of the family for all relatives at home, and the state in which each parent was born.

Even if you don't know the family's state of residence, you may still be able to locate the family by searching the 1880 Soundex for each Southern state. While the family's surname, Adams, was common, the first name of Newel was relatively uncommon, so your search should not be too difficult or tedious. A search through some of the recently published census indexes for 1860 and 1870 are other possibilities for learning the state of residence for families of this period.

While researching another line, you learn that your maternal grandmother, an eldest child, was born in New York around 1909, shortly after her parents emigrated from Germany. If you know the state in which the family lived in 1920, you should search that state's 1920 census index first. The 1920 census and its index provide the easiest way to track down this family. If you don't know where the family lived in 1920, you would need to research other sources to determine the family's residence, because the 1910 New York census is not yet indexed.

For instance, suppose you find a baby picture of your grandmother with the name and address of a New York City studio. You could study maps to find the specific borough in which the family may have lived in 1910. Then you could search the 1910 or 1920 census for names, ages, and relationships of all family members at home; language or dialect spoken; year of immigration; and the date family members were naturalized (1920 census only). The 1920 census also lists the city or province of origin for German immigrant respondents—and for their parents! If you find your grandmother on this census, you should be able to trace her ancestry across the Atlantic.

Meanwhile, a relative on your father's side of the family gives you a photocopy of your grandmother's 1922 obituary notice, which provides her age (fifty-two) and place of death. With this information, you can send to the state in which she died for her death certificate, which lists both her maiden name, Higglesworth, and her birthplace, Warwickshire, England.

You can now attempt to order a copy of your grandmother's birth certificate from St. Catherine's House, the repository for English and Welsh vital records dating back to July 1837. Birth certificates normally provide parents' names (including the mother's maiden name); the child's name, birth date, and birthplace; and the name of the person who supplied the information. (Note:

For a very common name, such as Mary Smith, you would need more detailed information—such as the exact date and place of birth—before ordering the birth certificate.)

Deciphering Archaic Records

As we have searched for information on our ancestors, we've found that reading records becomes easier as we become more experienced. We've learned how to interpret certain archaic terms and abbreviations, as well as how to deal with handwriting that is illegible.

Meaning Changes

Try to look up the word "diskette" in an older dictionary; you won't find it. Although "diskette" is a common word, its origin is very recent. Now look up the word "gay" and observe how much its meaning has changed in a relatively short time. As these examples illustrate, living languages are in a state of constant flux. Below, we explain some terms found in older records that modern researchers commonly misinterpret.

The term **in-law** once referred to relations that are now indicated by the term step- (as in step-son). If your ancestor's 1699 will names a "sonne-in-laue," you cannot assume that the document refers the man who married your ancestor's daughter; it may refer to the wife's son by a prior marriage (or even to both at the same time: It wasn't unknown for step-siblings to marry). If the will mentions several sons-in-law with the same surname, you can probably assume that they are what we call step-sons. By the same token, the woman we call a step-mother was then referred to as a mother-in-law. We have not found relations now termed parents-in-law called anything except **loving** or **well-beloved friends**. This phrase usually, though not always, indicated some relationship.

Cousin, niece, and **nephew,** and honorific titles such as **Mrs.** also had different meanings. About five centuries ago, **cousin** was a generic term for "relative." Some two-and-a-half centuries ago, the most common equivalent to the relations we now call cousins was niece or nephew—terms that were sometimes used to refer to aunts and uncles as well! Only within about the last one-and-a-half centuries has "cousin" referred exclusively to the children of your parents' siblings.

The words **niece** and **nephew** originated from the Latin terms for "granddaughter" and "grandson." Records dating back several centuries may employ these Latin-derived meanings. In later records, however, "niece" and "nephew" usually have the same meaning we associate with these terms today.

Mrs., an abbreviation of "mistress," denoted a woman of higher social class, and did not refer to her marital status until the eighteenth century. **Mr.**, an abbreviation of "master," likewise denoted a gentleman of a higher social class.

Junior and **senior** don't necessarily refer to father-son relationships; they were simply used to distinguish between individuals with the same name—the elder of the two was designated "Senior" and the younger, "Junior." If more than two individuals were involved, they may have been designated as follows: John Smith **Sr.**, John Smith **Jr.**, John Smith **Younger**, or **3rd**, and so on. Each John Smith would move up one niche when the John Smith older than he died or moved. Obviously, this method of identification can cause confusion for you, the researcher. To determine when, or if, the seniority designation changed periodically for these same-named individuals, you will probably need to find the death dates for each person.

Each area may have its own idiosyncratic naming practices. For instance, in early New England records, "brother" or "sister" may have referred to church friends rather than actual siblings. This was not generally true elsewhere in the U.S.

Legal terminology may also be confusing or misleading. The common term "My now wife," for instance, did not necessarily imply that a man had married previously. Rather, it simply protected the interests of his current wife and her descendants. To help you interpret wills and land records that contain difficult legal terminology, we have included a Glossary of Legal Terms at the end of this book. In some cases, you may also need a legal dictionary, such as *Black's Law Dictionary,* which defines both ancient and modern legal terminology.

Abbreviations and Latin Terms

LDS family history centers provide word lists that offer some helpful tips for deciphering records in languages other than English. You'll find the lists especially helpful for deciphering Latin, which was used in many early official English records. (See Chapter 4 for more information on the LDS family history centers.)

Abbreviations were quite common in early records; scribes often shortened both first and last names, Latin terms, and other frequently used words. The last few letters of the abbreviation were often written as superscript. "Jno" or "Jn°." and "Jas" or "Ja^s" were common abbreviations of John and James, respectively. Names such as Christopher, Christian, and Christianna were often shortened by using "X" to replace the "Christ" part of the name: "X^{ofer}" or "X," "X^n," and "X^{ianna}." "Do" and "d^o" are abbreviated forms of the commonly used "ditto."

Original records and published genealogies often contain abbreviations and Latin terms. Table 2-4 lists some we've found in English records.

Handwriting

Handwriting can be a problem. For example, the names David and Daniel look very similar in some older forms of handwriting. This means not only that you may have problems deciphering them yourself, but that a transcriber may have had trouble as well. Check under both names if you are using a transcribed record or index, and, to simplify your research, use primary records whenever possible. Because handwriting differences have evolved gradually, you can deal with this problem by beginning your research in the present and proceeding back one generation at a time.

If you're dealing with very old records, it may take considerable time and effort to decipher words, especially names, correctly. Consider asking someone more experienced to check your transcription. Two useful references for American research are Kirkham's *The Handwriting of American Records for a Period of 300 Years* and Stryker-Rodda's *Understanding Colonial Handwriting*. Jensen's *Genealogical Handbook of German Research* provides examples of early Germanic script, as well as translations of pertinent German terminology.

Table 2-4. Latin Abbreviations and Their Meanings

Abbreviation	Meaning
ae, aet.	at the age of
bp., ch.	baptism or christening
bur.	burial
c., ca.	circa (approximately)
C.T.A.	cum testemento annexo (with will attached)
D.B.	deed book
d.s.p.	died without issue
d.y.	died young
et al.	and others
et ux	and wife

Abbreviation	Meaning
inst. (instant)	same (as in this same month)
M.B.	marriage book
M.M.	Monthly Meeting (referring to Quaker church meetings)
O.B.	order book
O.S.	Old Style (referring to calendar; see Appendix B)
relict	widow or widower
s.a.	sans alliance (died unmarried)
sic	correct copy
twp.	township
ult. (ultimo)	past (as in the past month)
V.B.	vestry book
w.d.; w.p.	will dated; will proved

Be alert to changes in letter formation and punctuation. For example, through the eighteenth century many scribes used an archaic form of the lower case "s" which looks much like an "f," as in the name "Jesse" below:

Punctuation was seldom used and differed from today's usage. For instance, people used dots (or periods) to indicate both pauses and stops.

Spelling Variations
Search thoroughly for alternate spellings of both places and names. Because spelling has become standardized only recently (even lexicographers didn't agree on spelling until the last century or so), and because many people altered the spelling or pronunciation of their names and birth places when they immigrated to America, you may find a variety of similar surnames and places of origin that you can trace to a common ancestor.

Place names

Expect to find differences between the current spellings of place names and spellings you obtain from family or other records. To help sort out possibilities, consider all instances in which your ancestor referred to a birthplace. Because family lore concerning immigrants' birthplaces is often wrong, you'll need to conduct thorough research. According to Mokotoff and Sack's *Where Once We Walked: Jewish Communities in Eastern Europe,* if immigrants came from a town with a long or difficult name, families may have passed down an easier or more familiar name, perhaps one mentioned by the ancestor.

Surnames

Many American surnames are variants of immigrants' original surnames. Through the nineteenth century especially, social pressure led many immigrants to Anglicize names that sounded "foreign." In most cases, these names were Germanic or Slavic. Thus, in looking for a Brown, Black, Carpenter, McInturf, Price, Peterson, or Noah, keep your mind open to such possible original forms as Braun, Schwartz, Zimmerman, Muckendorf, Preiss, Bieter, or Noahkowski. Helpful references for spelling variations include Jones' *German-American Names,* Hanks and Hodges' *A Dictionary of Surnames,* and the appendix to *A Century of Population Growth, 1790-1900* (a reprint of a Bureau of the Census document).

You cannot always rely on names; people who use different spellings of a surname may be related, while those who use the same spelling may not be. For instance, our surname, Cosgriff, is derived from the Gaelic Coscraigh. However, in old Ireland, literacy was uncommon and spelling was not standardized. So, depending on the local dialect, personal preference, or the whim of the recorder, the name could be written as Cosgrove, Cossgroove, Cosgrave, Cosgriff, Clusker, Cluskey, Cosgreve, Cosgreave, Cosgrive, Cusko, Cusker, Cuskery, Coskeran, Coskr, Coskerry, Crosgrave, McCoskery, McCoskrerey, McCusker, O'Coskery, and so on. In the U.S., it is occasionally written with an initial "K," as in Kosgrove. Moreover, these variants are unrelated to the English surname Cosgrove, which has a completely different origin. As you research, you may find that in some families, each branch may have developed its own pronunciation and spelling of its surname.

You may find a few family names for which spelling remains consistent. In some of these cases, you can trace ancestral lines more easily than lines that contain several alternate spellings of a surname. If you find a group of Heywardes that consistently spells the name the same way, while a nearby group contains various or haphazard spellings, these families may be unrelated. On the other hand, they may simply have had different rates of literacy or different parish clerks.

We cannot overemphasize the importance of searching for all variant spellings of your family names. *More than any other single reason, taking inadequate precautions for spelling variations leads to failure in family-tree research.* Even the most informative records do you no good if they are filed under Unsmun and Eintsmen, and you check only for Heinzeman.

We have found some patterns in spelling variations for names beginning with certain letters. Below are some suggestions for finding all alternate spellings for these names.

- **Names that begin with a vowel or an "H":** Look for alternate spellings under each vowel (including combinations and substitutes). For example, Argyle might also be spelled Ergoll, Eargle, Eigle, Irgle, Urgull, Orgle, Oargel, Yargell, or Jurgell; variants of Hackerman may include Ackerman, Eckemman, Eickmann, Ikeman, Oeckerman, or Uckleman.

- **Names that begin with one or more consonants:** Look first for alternate consonant-vowel combinations; for example, for the name Branson, search also for Brenson, Brinson, Bronson, and Brunson. Next, look for names that contain additional letters, such as Brainson, Brandtson, Bhrandsen, Berantsen, Brannison. Finally, to make sure you don't overlook any alternative form, search every name that begins with the given consonant.

- **Names with prefixes:** In addition, you should consider other initial (or beginning) letters for names containing prefixes that may have been added or deleted, or names whose initial letters sound similar to another letter. In the earlier Cosgriff example, we found spelling variants under four initial letters—C, K, M, and O. Locational prefixes such as Van and Vander (Dutch); Le, La, De, and Du (French); Am, Zu, and Zum (German); and Da, Di, Dal, Del, and Della (Italian), were sometimes retained, sometimes dropped, and sometimes changed. Thus, to find the Vanderbilt, Zumwalt, and duPlessis families on a census, you may need to check the Soundex under Bilt, Walt, and Plessis.

Finding Professional Researchers

Depending upon your research goals and your ability or willingness to achieve them on your own, you may want to enlist the help of an expert. Even if you don't receive regular professional assistance, you should discuss your progress and plans with a more experienced researcher periodically. If you associate with a local genealogical society or an online bulletin board (see Chapter 11), you'll meet people who can help you.

Many societies and libraries can supply you with lists of local professional researchers. Probably the best of these lists is the *List of Persons Certified* supplied by the Board of Certification of Genealogists. This non-profit organization certifies genealogical competence in the following categories: Certified Genealogist, Genealogical Record Searcher, American Lineage Specialist (for patriotic societies), American Indian Lineage Specialist, Genealogical Lecturer, and Genealogical Instructor. You can obtain a current list by sending $3.00, a note stating your needs, a long (#10) envelope, and 78 cents postage to the following address:

Board for Certification of Genealogists
P.O. Box 14291
Washington, D.C. 20044

You can also obtain a list of genealogists accredited by the LDS Family History Library by writing to the library at 35 North West Temple Street, Salt Lake City, Utah 84150 (include a SASE), or to any family history center. The LDS Family History Library maintains and reissues two lists every three months: One for the United States and Canada, and one for other countries.

Another resource—which may be available at your library—is the *Directory of Professional Genealogists,* published in 1993 at Salt Lake City, Utah by the Association of Professional Genealogists (APG). The directory lists hundreds of APG members and their areas of expertise. For individuals the directory costs $15.00, but libraries can receive it free. If your library doesn't have a copy, you can ask a librarian to order it.

Association of Professional Genealogists
3421 M Street N.W., Suite 236
Washington, D.C. 20007

Keeping and Filing Notes

You may be surprised at how rapidly you accumulate data. This growing collection of data is only useful if you can find specific facts when you need them. To do this, you must have not only accurate records, but also a good filing system.

Computers, of course, offer the most efficient means of organizing information. However, computers can't magically organize a messy system that is full of inaccuracies. You should organize your research before you computerize it.

There is probably no "best" record-keeping system. Any method will do as long as it fulfills the following criteria:

• Offers easy retrieval of information

- Enables meticulous documentation of all research information

- Is reasonably simple to use and maintain

Record-Keeping Suggestions

The following ideas apply to all record-keeping systems, whether computerized or not.

- **Hand-written notes:** Unless you have a portable computer and are very proficient at using it, you'll need to take some long-hand notes. Keep notes on notebook (8.5" x 11") or legal-sized (8.5" x 14") paper. Use the same size paper for your note-keeping as for your genealogical forms. Avoid recording information on scraps of paper, envelope backs, and checkbook stubs; such odd-sized items mysteriously disappear.

  Use only one side of the paper to record your notes; when you need to spread your notes in front of you to find a particular piece of information, your search will be more efficient and less frustrating if you don't have to flip each paper over to see whether the information you need is on the back side.

- **Abbreviations:** Especially if you are a beginner, it is better to record too much than too little. Hasty abbreviation often leads to mistakes, omissions, and illegibility.

- **Photocopies:** Whenever possible, photocopy the records you need. Some courthouses, archives, and other public record centers may charge more for their photocopy services than libraries charge; obtain fee information in advance. Remember to identify the source somewhere on the photocopy; if you're copying pages of a book or magazine, photocopy the title page as well. For courthouse sources, be sure to record the courthouse, office, binder, and so on.

- **Abstracts:** Once you've gained enough experience to know what is or isn't useful, abstract: That is, take from documents only data of possible value. This can save time, effort, and frustration when you're dealing with long, wordy legal documents, such as land or probate records.

  Strive to be meticulous. A book reference, for instance, should include page number(s) and full bibliographic information (title, author, name and place of publisher, date of publication, library, and call number). Try to review your notes and compare them with the original source before you leave the library or archive to ensure that you have written legible, accurate, complete information.

- **Inadequacies in records:** If, while searching the 1870 microfilmed census of Horry County, South Carolina, you find many pages so faded that they are illegible, you should note that fact along with the data you gather. This will suggest a possible reason for your inability to find some of the information you expected from the records. Make such notes of any entry that is difficult to read or interpret.

- **Research scope:** We have noticed a tendency among beginners to focus exclusively upon direct lines, whereas more experienced researchers have learned the value of collecting collateral lines. In some cases, of course, a more direct approach saves time and is sufficient. However, where vital facts are hard to come by, recording and then sorting an entire community can be helpful. If you assemble such databases as you conduct your research, you can deposit them in several places, including Ancestral File (see Chapter 4), where others can access your findings.

Organizing Your Notes

To make your research efficient and worthwhile, you must develop an organized filing system for the information you collect and analyze. We have developed a relatively simple note-filing system that may help you as you begin your own research. It is a paper-based system; while it provides a logical and succinct method of data organization and storage, it is more time-consuming and tedious to maintain than a computer-based system would be.

With a few obvious modifications (such as using computer files rather than 8.5"x 11" manila folders to store notes), this system works even better on a computer. Because computers reduce the time and space requirements associated with data use and storage, and because they enable easier manipulation of information, they can simplify the filing process and enhance your ability to access the information you need.

Our note-filing system organizes your research into family files, correspondence logs, document files, research agendas, research summaries, and miscellaneous files.

Family File

Keep information and notes in a letter- or legal-sized manila folder. Begin by keeping all information on one branch of your family (the Jones branch, for example) in one folder. When that folder grows fat, so that locating information becomes time-consuming, divide its contents into separate folders for each family (for example, the John Jones family and the Ken Jones family).

Keep family folders in alphabetical order according to surname. Alphabetize within that surname according to husbands' first names. Use the husband's name, birth date, death date, and residence as identification on the folder tab. This way, if you have several heads of families with identical names (three John Joneses, for instance), you can arrange them chronologically, filing the youngest person first: John JONES, Boston, Massachusetts 1827-1876; John JONES, Boston, Massachusetts 1801-1837; John JONES, Boston, Massachusetts 1778-18??. This system makes it simple to locate any family within your set of files.

If the family you're researching lived in more than one place, you may want to keep a separate folder for each location. This is another way to divide the bulk when research notes start accumulating for one family.

Research Summary

After each research session, summarize your findings in writing. Your dated entries should include discoveries and implications. Ask such questions as, "What facts or clues have I found?", "How do these fit with the information I already had?", and "What additional research sources would be helpful in light of today's findings?" Write down your ideas, then act upon the answers. Writing a research summary ensures rigorous analysis each time you conduct research.

By keeping your research summaries current, you will be able to progress logically and efficiently, without repeating research. In addition, if for some reason you don't complete the research, these summaries will enable another researcher to easily determine what you accomplished and how to proceed. You can sleep better knowing your research system is straightforward and self-explanatory.

Research Agenda

Your research agenda plays an important role in your note-keeping system. (Some genealogy texts refer to this agenda as a calendar or log.) You begin this agenda when you write down your research goals for each name you decide to research. After writing your goals, make four columns on your paper (see Figure 2-1). In the first column, briefly describe the sources you intend to search or have already searched. (Later chapters and appendices will help you determine specific sources to list in this column.) In the second column, state the purpose of your search. In the third, write the date you searched the source(s). In the last column, record the results (for example, "Nothing found," or "See notes p. 5"). Keep your agenda current and at the front of your research notes to provide a convenient and useful index to your research.

Research Agenda: Cyrus Brown/Mary Funk
Goals: Find birth dates/places and parents

Source: Description or Location	Purpose of Search	Date	Results
Land Recs (DB#2) Probate Recs (WB#1) Rye, KS	Date came to KS; Whence; Date of Cyrus' Death	9 Jul 1990	Photocopy in Document File
1900/1910 censuses Freeland Co, CO micro#456123	Birth dates/places of Mary, her parents & children; when md James	15 Aug 1990	Extracts pp. 1-4
HARD ROCK RECORDS by Bigler (929/B2) in Rye Public Library	Any family data	12 Sep 1990	Nil; wrong time period
Brown family Bible in possession of Diane Showalter	Vital statistics: names, dates, places	19 Sep 1990	Photocopy in Document File

Figure 2-1. Example of a Research Agenda

Correspondence Log

Be consistent in your efforts to write letters, and keep good records of correspondence. One method is to attach a carbon copy or photocopy of your original letter to its reply. Give both letters the same identifying number: The first letter you send is #1, and #1A is the letter you receive in reply; the second letter you send is #2, and #2A is the reply. Keep all letters attached to a correspondence log, illustrated in Figure 2-2. Keep one log in each family's folder. If you prefer, you can integrate your correspondence log into your research agenda.

# and Date Sent	Name/Address	Purpose/Request	Answer Date
#1. 15 Mar 1990	Mrs. James Hoy, 456 Palm St., Hemet, CA	Sent chart to get information in her possession	30 Apr 1990
#2. 30 Mar 1990	County Clerk, Rocky Pt., KS	Land/probate entries: Brown, Read, and Funk	6 Jun 1990

Figure 2-2. Correspondence Log for Cyrus Brown and Mary Funk

Writing effective letters
One of the great advantages of researching today is the ease and speed of communication. You can reach individuals, organizations, databases, and information centers by telephone, fax, and modem, as well as through the traditional mail system. This is fortunate, since correspondence is essential for accessing record sources. Indeed, effective communication may advance your genealogical search as much as any other single factor; but effective communication does not come naturally to most of us. The principles explained below can help you get the information you need as you trace your roots.

Before you draft a letter, clearly define the specific information you want, then determine who can most likely furnish those facts. Learn something about the organization or individual to whom you are writing—services provided, fees charged, and so on—before you write. The following "C"'s will make your letters more effective:

• Clear expression

• Concise wording

• Convincing tone

• Courteous style

• Correct usage (spelling, grammar, etc.)

• Clean appearance

Keep your communications short and simple. Avoid form letters; however, fill-in-the-blank questionnaires or simple charts are often helpful. Relatives may enjoy family news; otherwise, stick to the point (and resist the temptation to explain your pedigree problems to overworked clerks). Ask for one piece of information at a time, especially the first time you write, unless several facts are located in the same source. Also, make a habit of requesting names and addresses of others who may be able to help you.

When addressing envelopes, use titles for public officials to avoid having letters forwarded in case of transfers. Write in the native language if possible, and do your homework regarding customs in the country to which you're sending your letters. After you've sent your inquiry, expect long delays—often months, rather than weeks—unless you're communicating online; if the organization has an Internet address, your search could possibly be finished within minutes.

Fees and SASEs
Include a self-addressed, stamped envelope (SASE) for domestic mail and international postal reply coupons for international mail, except when dealing with organizations that charge fees. Send sufficient payment (use checks, money orders, or bank drafts) to cover expenses. If you are not certain of the charges, estimate or offer to pay when you receive an invoice. Genealogists who succeed in obtaining information from churches usually include a donation (perhaps with the explanation, "In memory of my ____ ancestors").

Document File
Documents are original records. You may keep them in the appropriate family folder or in a separate file. (If you're working on a computer, you will need this file to be paper-based unless you use a scanner to copy the documents into your computer.) In addition to original documents, the document file may be a good place to store items such old books, original letters, audio- and video-tapes of interviews of family members, and other items that you aren't able to file in your computer.

Let's suppose you obtain a photocopy of an ancestor's will from a courthouse. After abstracting and recording pertinent data for the family folder, you may want to place the document in a separate document file for safe-keeping. To ensure easy retrieval, you can arrange this file alphabetically by surname so it matches the family file. Be sure to cross-index the document if it contains information on more than one family. For instance, if your Jones document or folder contains information pertaining to your Showalter and Funk families, note that fact in all three files.

It may be useful to keep all documents in a single folder and give each document a number. Then, in source listings on family group sheets and other materials, you can record the document number. You can also create an alphabetical index of people referred to in these documents. The Research Data Filer provided with the Personal Ancestral File (Chapter 4) has this capability.

Miscellaneous Files
Keep separate file folders for other categories as needed—for example, "Research Ideas," or "Geography: Early Massachusetts" (for maps and gazetteer excerpts), or "Future Sources," to record potentially helpful sources for branches of the family that you have not yet begun to investigate.

Summary
You can organize research notes, documents, and letters as follows: Keep a manila folder for each family, identified on the folder tab by the husband's name, life dates, and residence. The family folder contains the following items:

1. Research summary sheets

2. Research agenda, followed by research notes

3. Correspondence log, followed by letters (which you've identified by number)

4. Documents for the family, if desired (you may file all documents in a separate, alphabetized file)

Bibliography

General

Szucs, Loretto Dennis, and Sandra Hargreaves Luebking, eds. *The Source: A Guidebook of American Genealogy*. Rev. ed. Salt Lake City, UT: Ancestry, 1996.

Boundary Changes

Eichholz, Alice, ed. *Ancestry's Red Book: American State, County and Town Sources*. Rev. ed. Salt Lake City, UT: Ancestry, 1992. Emphasis is on genealogical record holdings of all U.S. counties, which are extensively covered. Also supplies names of parent counties. Comprehensive coverage of the county court, town, census, and other important genealogical holdings in the U.S.

Long, John H., ed. *Atlas of Historical County Boundaries*. New York, NY: Simon and Schuster, 1992-present. A series that provides extensive boundary information. This multi-volume atlas explains and maps in documented detail all changes taking place in each U.S. county dating back to its formation. Includes references to legislation that adjusted county lines for the benefit of a landowner named in the legislation, usually to keep a land parcel intact to simplify tax collection. While such cases were exceptional, some Southern states had several; most notable was Tennessee (with more than five hundred). Most states will be covered separately in this series, except for the smallest ones, which will be combined with an adjacent state.

Thorndale, William, and William Dollarhide. *Map Guide to the U.S. Federal Censuses 1790-1920*. Baltimore, MD: Genealogical Publishing Co., 1992. Reprint. Contains the first complete set of maps showing evolution of U.S. county boundaries. Includes almost four hundred individual state maps, as well as facts about censuses and tips about census-searching.

Geography

Abate, Frank R., ed. *Omni Gazetteer of the United States*. Detroit, MI: Omnigraphics, 1991. Versions in both print and CD-ROM. The printed version contains nine regional volumes and a separate volume indexing the more than 1.5 million place names, which include counties, cities, towns, islands, rivers, swamps, creeks, historic buildings, churches, cemeteries, and other facilities and structures.

Lewis, Samuel A. *A Topographical Dictionary of England*. London: 1831, 1833, et al. Available in microfiche; Salt Lake City, UT: Traditions, 1977.

Indispensable. Part of the Microfiche Reference Collections at LDS family history centers. Dictionaries are also available for Scotland, Wales, and Ireland.

Parker, J. Carlyle, ed. *Library Service for Genealogists*. Detroit, MI: Gale Research Co., 1981. "A selected bibliography of statewide place name literature, old gazetteers, postal service histories, ghost town directories and histories, and boundary change guides." Quite good; listed by state.

Handwriting Problems

Jensen, Larry O. *Genealogical Handbook of German Research*. 2 vols. Pleasant Grove, UT: 1978-83. Jensen Publications, P.O. Box 441, Pleasant Grove, UT 84062, tel. 801-785-4582. Good help for German genealogical research techniques and sources, including help with handwritten records. A microfiche copy of this book is available in the "Microfiche Reference Collections" at LDS family history centers.

Kirkham, E. Kay. *The Handwriting of American Records for a Period of 300 Years*. Logan, UT: Everton Publishers, 1973. Techniques for reading old handwriting, abbreviations, etc. Quite helpful.

Stryker-Rodda, Harriet. *Understanding Colonial Handwriting*. Baltimore, MD: Genealogical Publishing Co., 1986. Helpful, but less thorough than Kirkham's.

Legal Terms

Black's Law Dictionary. St. Paul, MN: West Publishing Co., 1991.

Place Names

Mokotoff, Gary, and Sallyann Sack. *Where Once We Walked: Jewish Communities in Eastern Europe*. Teaneck, NJ: Avotaynu, 1991. This gazetteer should help those with roots in east Europe, where place names can be particularly difficult. Compiled as a guide to the Jewish communities destroyed in the Holocaust, it will aid others as well. It contains some 22,000 towns, along with 15,000 alternate, usually older, place names.

Surnames

Hanks, Patrick, and Flavia Hodges. *A Dictionary of Surnames*. New York, NY: Oxford University Press, 1989. A more comprehensive reference than Jones. It is the first systematic comparative survey of surnames, based on intensive research in all the major European languages (especially good for Jewish, Iberian, and Gaelic names). In addition to pinpointing the linguistic derivation and meaning of each name, it offers many historical facts. Also, its comprehensive index will help you determine first names and nicknames, so you can easily determine that "Giotto" is a diminutive of "Francis," for example, while "Nanni" is a cognate of "John." You can use this as a reference when trying to track down a particular nickname.

Jones, George F. *German-American Names.* Baltimore, MD: Genealogical Publishing Co., 1990. An excellent book. Covers almost 13,000 names. Introduction has good material on significance, origin, and Americanization of German names.

Sowell, Thomas. *Immigrant America.* New York, NY: Basic Books, 1981. A popular, fun-to-read work. We recommend this book for valuable, interesting background information (cultural, occupational, personality patterns, etc.) for the largest American immigration groups: Irish, Scotch-Irish, German, Italian, Jewish, Japanese, Chinese, Hispanic, and African and other black groups. Contrary to the popularly accepted "melting pot" myth, there was a strong tendency for most ethnic groups to marry among themselves, usually for at least the first couple of generations following immigration.

Steward, George R. *American Given Names.* New York, NY: Oxford University Press, 1979.

U.S. Bureau of the Census. *A Century of Population Growth, 1790-1900.* Reprint. New York, NY: Johnson Reprints, 1966. This book has a valuable appendix that lists surname variations in the 1790 census.

Woodcock, Thomas, and John M. Robinson. *The Oxford Guide to Heraldry.* New York, NY: Oxford University Press, 1988. Provides good information on this topic, using coats-of-arms to help trace families. Includes a chapter on America in addition to sections on each of the European nations.

Chapter 3

Evaluating Evidence

Learning to use and evaluate evidence properly is a necessity for successful research. A small but well-substantiated collection of genealogical findings will be much more satisfying to your posterity and to successive researchers than a large but inaccurate pedigree would be. To ensure accuracy, you should use direct and primary evidence whenever possible. If this is not possible, use secondary and circumstantial evidence taken from every available source and keep your conclusions tentative: In your notes, use wording such as, "It appears from these sources . . ." or, "Thus, it may be . . . ." Such precautions may seem difficult or tedious, but by being consistently cautious when drawing conclusions, you may forestall many errors.

Your ability to evaluate printed sources will increase as you gain experience in using original records. As a way to gain a feel for the reliability of printed sources, we suggest that you study classic works pertaining to the area of your interest (as recommended by librarians, experienced genealogists, or appropriate bibliographies).

Types Of Evidence

There are four basic categories of evidence: primary, secondary, direct, and circumstantial. Each type of evidence provides a different degree of reliability. For each piece of data you find, you should ascertain which type of evidence the source of the data offers. This will help you determine whether the information is accurate, or, if you find records with conflicting data, which record is most reliable.

Primary

Primary evidence is recorded at the time of the event, or very closely thereafter, by a trustworthy witness. If a birth certificate, for example, was prepared shortly after the birth of a child and signed by the doctor or midwife who delivered the child, the birth certificate can be considered primary and direct evidence for the individual's birth date, birthplace, mother, and father (except, perhaps, in the case of an illegitimate birth). A church marriage record noted by the minister who performed the ceremony provides primary and direct evidence of that event.

We would prefer to prove all our genealogical hypotheses with primary and direct evidence; however, that is not always possible. Often we must use other sources.

Secondary

Secondary evidence is information that was either provided by an individual with no personal knowledge of the event in question, or taken from an earlier record. For example, if the birth certificate mentioned above included parental ages and birthplaces, this information would be secondary rather than primary evidence, because these dates concern events that occurred decades earlier. As this example illustrates, one document can be a source of both primary and secondary evidence.

A family Bible in which marriage and birth notations have been made may provide primary evidence, but it often falls in the category of secondary evidence if the reliable witnesses to the event (usually the parents) recorded the dates some time after they occurred. In some cases, you can determine whether the notation should be considered primary or secondary: If the color of ink is the same for all entries, they were probably recorded at the same time, rather than as the events occurred; if the publication date of the Bible is later than some or all of the dates, you know that they were recorded some time after they occurred.

Another example of secondary evidence is an event recorded at the time of its occurrence, but by a person other than an eyewitness. For example, while searching through some old family letters, you find one postmarked July 10, 1908, New Haven, Connecticut, signed by a Calvin Hendricks and addressed to a Lona Fewens of St. Louis, Missouri. The salutation reads, "Dear Sister," and the letter congratulates her on the birth of her son William two weeks previous. This letter supplies secondary, although direct (see below), evidence for the birth date of the child.

Secondary evidence also includes records made some years after the event by someone who was not an eyewitness to the event. A pension application completed by the widow of a Revolutionary War veteran, for instance, might include the veteran's birth date. How much credibility do we assign to this information? Because the widow presumably was not an eyewitness to her husband's birth, and the event occurred a lifetime before her statement, this is secondary evidence; if it conflicts with a birth date found in a town or church register, you would record the latter date, because it is based on better evidence.

If the widow supplies a marriage date as part of this same pension file, that date may also be unreliable. Federal legislation during some periods required the widow of a Revolutionary War veteran to have married him prior to his military service to be eligible for a pension. If the widow applied during one of these periods, she may have purposefully supplied an incorrect marriage date. Thus, you would regard this witness as possibly untrustworthy, and the resulting evidence as suspect.

Direct

Direct evidence, as the name suggests, answers a question directly. A birth certificate that states the parents' names and the time and place of the child's birth provides direct evidence of the child's parentage, birth date, and birthplace. A dated notation of marriage in someone's journal also provides direct evidence for the names of the participants and their marriage date.

Circumstantial

The letter mentioned above that was written by Calvin Hendricks to his sister provides an example of circumstantial, rather than direct, evidence for Mrs. Fewens' maiden name. Although the letter contains no statement that Lona Fewens' maiden name was Hendricks, you may assume this because Calvin Hendricks calls her his sister.

Circumstantial evidence can sometimes lead you to direct evidence. If you search the St. Louis marriage records, you might discover the 1907 marriage license for William Fewens and Lona Hendricks, which would provide direct evidence of her maiden name. If the marriage license is for William Fewens and Lona Hardwick, you can hypothesize that perhaps she had been married before, that Calvin Hendricks was perhaps a half-brother, or that the clerk who completed the license misspelled the bride's maiden name.

The letter written by Calvin Hendricks also provides circumstantial evidence that Connecticut may have been a prior residence of the Hendricks family. You need to research New Haven records to substantiate that guess. (The information on Lona's marriage record would lead you to search for Hardwick as well as Hendricks.)

When direct, primary sources are lacking, you must rely upon circumstantial or secondary evidence. In these cases, you must analyze your research more rigorously and substantiate it with additional sources. If such detective work hasn't yet become a strong point for you, try to work with someone who is more knowledgeable. At the very least, find someone willing to play "devil's advocate" as you formulate hypotheses, or listen to yourself think aloud as you try to work out difficult family-tree problems. A patient relative or friend may be helpful as a sounding-board. The responses of an objective listener may also provide a useful perspective.

To protect yourself from drawing incorrect conclusions when using circumstantial evidence, use one or both of the following approaches:

Find Additional Sources

In the Hendricks-Fewens example, we looked for a marriage license to prove a relationship that we deduced from circumstantial evidence. We also searched for the will of Calvin Hendricks' father to see whether it mentioned a daughter or stepdaughter named Lona. In addition, we examined the 1900 New Haven census for all Hendricks and Hardwick families, as we suspected that the family might have lived there. (We searched the 1900 census because it is indexed, but the 1910 census—which is not indexed—may be an even better source of information.)

Try To Disprove Your Case

If you are looking for the parents of an ancestor named Robert Wilson, who was born in the county of Aberdeen, Scotland, you may be tempted to conclude your search upon finding a christening record for a Robert Wilson in the correct place and period. However, many serious genealogical errors occur because inexperienced researchers don't consider the likelihood of there being (in this case, probably many) contemporaries with the same name as an ancestor. To avoid identifying the wrong individual, and consequently the wrong set of parents, as your ancestors, ask yourself questions such as the following:

- **Could the Robert Wilson I found in my research have died before he married?** Look through the burial records of his church to find out. If he died as a baby or a young boy, he obviously was not your ancestor.

- **Were there contemporary Wilson families in the area who were also having children?** Check out not only the rest of the register in which you found the first entry, but also the registers of the nearby parishes, as well as non-conformist registers, and check any other available records to learn of candidate Wilson families whose children may not have been baptized. (The *Index to the Old Parochial Registers of Scotland* described in Chapter 4 enables you to check out most such possibilities in a matter of minutes.)

If you find other Robert Wilsons christened in Aberdeen around the same time as the first, you must conduct further research to determine which is most likely your ancestor. (In the case of a less common name, you might be safe in concluding that the individual for whom you find a christening record is probably your ancestor.)

Conflicting Facts

As a general rule, choose primary evidence over secondary evidence. For conflicting secondary evidence, choose the more trustworthy source or the one made closer to the time of the event. If primary evidence conflicts, record both sources and note the following information: All pertinent data from both sources; all discrepancies; a description of the problem; and your reasons for choosing to use evidence in one source rather than the other.

If a number of sources offer conflicting information, it often helps to make a table in which you list the sources in one column and the information from those sources in the other. Figure 3-1 illustrates a table you might create if various sources provide conflicting information for an ancestor's birth year.

Source	Birth Year Recorded or Deduced
death certificate	1876
obituary notice	1878
family Bible (published 1884)	1873
Uncle Ed (by his memory)	1874
1880 census	1872

Figure 3-1. Example of a Discrepancy Table

In this example, the death certificate and obituary notice were recorded a full lifetime after the birth. We'll say Uncle Ed gave you his information even later. The entry in the family Bible can't be considered primary evidence because its publication date is more than a decade after the recorded birth year. The entry there, however, was made closer to the time of birth than any of the other sources, except the 1880 census. But that census records only age, not birth date. Therefore, because the family Bible provides direct, secondary evidence, you would consider it the best source available; probably even better than the census with its circumstantial evidence. (As this example illustrates, the earliest evidence is not necessarily the best.)

Dating Analysis

Are you good at arithmetic? The connection between arithmetic and genealogy might not seem obvious, but anybody who has tried to reconstruct family lines from sparse data and conflicting dates can appreciate its importance. At every stage of research, you should consider the question, "Does the chronology make sense?" For example, a person of European descent born in 1842 obviously did not marry in 1851, and a woman older than fifty years of age is extremely unlikely to have borne children.

Knowing the birth years of children can help you approximate their mother's year of birth. If the children were born during a twenty-year period, you can guess that the mother was about twenty-five years old when her first child was born. However, if the first birth (or first several births) was a stillbirth or miscarriage, it may not have been recorded; in such cases, the mother may be significantly older than you may assume from her children's birth records. Also, if the child-bearing period of one wife covers much more than twenty-five years, or if some of the children's birth dates fall within nine months of one another, you must investigate the possibility that more than one wife or couple of the same name is involved.

Of course, local and ethnic marriage customs vary. For example, in Ireland from 1870 through the early 1900s, individuals married both less often and later than any other Europeans; the Irish were typically married after the age of thirty rather than before. Our research suggests that this tendency persisted in America at least into the early nineteenth century. Appalachian brides and grooms, on the other hand, have always tended to marry very early—as early as thirteen or fourteen years of age.

In researching colonial English, Scottish, and German immigrants and their descendants through several generations, we have rarely found a groom younger than eighteen years of age, though brides were often as young as sixteen, and occasionally fifteen. While not typical, neither was it uncommon for a groom to be twenty to thirty years older than his bride, especially if he was a widower. In seventeenth-century Virginia, we have found records of a few brides aged eleven—proving that there are exceptions to all genealogical generalities. (The unusual and bizarre was as fascinating to our ancestors as it is to us; the further such exceptions varied from the norm, the more newsworthy they were. Our favorite case in point was reported in a March 1771 newspaper in Richmond, Virginia: "William Carter, third son of John Carter, aged 23, married Mrs. Sarah Ellyson, relict of Gerard Ellyson, aged 85, a sprightly old Tit with £3000 fortune, yesterday in Henrico Co.")

Wills often indicate or imply children's ages; for example, "I bequeath to my loving daughter Mary when she reaches age fourteen . . . ." However, in some early colonial wills, both grandchildren and great-grandchildren are referred to as grandchildren. In these instances, you could easily miscalculate individuals' ages if you weren't careful to find primary evidence. The average

age between generations is about thirty years; if you can find no other clues, you may need to use that figure to make estimations.

Chapter 7 of this book discusses other facts you may find in public or family records that can help you determine your ancestors' birth dates. If you're doing eighteenth-century British or colonial American research, or sixteenth- and seventeenth-century European research, Appendix B: Calendar Changes may help you avoid making mistakes in determining dates.

Bibliography

Greenwood, Val D. *The Researcher's Guide to American Genealogy*. 2nd ed. Baltimore, MD: Genealogical Publishing Co., 1990.

Harland, Derek. *Genealogical Research Standards*. Salt Lake City, UT: Bookcraft, 1970.

National Society of the Daughters of the American Revolution. *Is that Lineage Right?* Washington, DC, 1982.

Rubincam, Milton. *Pitfalls in Genealogical Research*. Salt Lake City, UT: Ancestry, 1987.

Stevenson, Noel C. *Genealogical Evidence. A Guide to the Standard of Proof Relating to Pedigrees, Ancestry, Heirship, and Family History*. Laguna Hills, CA: Aegean Press, 1979.

Stratton, Eugene. "The Validity of Genealogical Evidence." *National Genealogical Quarterly*, vol. 72, Dec. 1984.

Chapter 4

Sources of Information: Libraries

Until recently, sources of information about families may have been few in number and difficult to access. We now face a far different challenge—dealing effectively with information overload as technology makes it possible to access formerly difficult-to-obtain information at increasingly rapid rates. Unfortunately, this technology also makes it easier to squander valuable time and effort wandering among thousands of information sources. Now more than ever, you need a solid basic knowledge of where and how to locate relevant sources. Try to become familiar with the simple library techniques explained in this chapter, and establish a good working relationship with your local reference librarian, with whom you should check often about newly acquired books, microcollections, and databases.

Library collections of local histories, family histories, genealogies, bibliographies, maps, and atlases are treasure-houses for family historians. Almost every nation, state, and province has at least one large repository (such as a state archive) for many of its early records. Szucs and Luebking's *The Source* lists each of the fifty state archives.

Large public or university libraries may also house excellent sources. Dallas, Denver, San Francisco, Los Angeles, Atlanta, Fort Wayne, Seattle, and New York have public libraries with especially large genealogical collections. The Sutro Library in San Francisco and the Newberry Library in Chicago also have excellent collections.

Some libraries are completely devoted to genealogy. Among these are the Daughters of the American Revolution Libraries in Washington, D.C., Oklahoma City, Oklahoma, and Alliance, Nebraska; and the Filson Club Library in Louisville, Kentucky. The LDS Family History Library, operated by The Church of Jesus Christ of Latter-day Saints (or LDS church), in Salt Lake City, Utah, with its interconnected branch system of family history centers, is especially good. Also, you shouldn't overlook small collections in or near ancestral hometowns; depending on the area, these may prove to be the most helpful of all.

Library Research

Some libraries provide pamphlets or bibliographies listing their genealogical sources. Some also provide instruction sheets for genealogical research, with special emphasis on their collections. If you must travel some distance to research a collection, try to locate and study such guides beforehand. Contact the library to determine whether a guide is available and how to obtain it.

We do much of our research at a large university library. Although we have never seen it listed as an especially good genealogical repository, and it does not have a specific genealogy section, we know it contains a wealth of research material, especially for Virginia. Most large academic and public libraries do have many useful genealogical resources; however, many genealogists lack the skills to make library searching productive.

Students in our genealogy classes express great satisfaction when they learn how to explore on their own the many genealogical materials available at the library. Because guided tours provide a quick way to learn about the contents of a particular collection, you should ask about tours at any library in which you expect to do much research. You may also want to enlist the help of a friend, family member, or cooperative local librarian to teach you how to use the pertinent indexes, catalogs (card and online), and special collections.

Using Card Catalogs and Indexes

There are three basic methods for looking up references in catalogs—by author, by title, and by subject. Some genealogical libraries also allow you to look up references under locality and/or surname. If you're new to genealogical research, you should begin searching by subject (and locality and surname if available). Find these sections of the catalog and look up the surname, location, or any other subject for which you need information. A list of suggested subject headings is provided at the end of this chapter.

Most large libraries use online or microfiche catalogs instead of card catalogs. Automated systems can simplify your research, especially among large collections. The quality of online catalogs varies—if you find the system at your local library difficult to use, try others. Chapter 11 explains how you can explore hundreds of library catalogs from your home using a computer and a modem.

All major libraries house indispensable subject and name indexes covering sources as diverse as census records, newspaper obituaries, and published and unpublished journals and manuscripts. Check with a librarian periodically to find out about new indexes that you may be able to use in your research. Also, local and state genealogical societies are doing an excellent job of gathering pertinent and often widely scattered materials for publication in their periodicals.

Indexes found at the end of books can also be helpful, but you should not rely on them. To make the best use of any indexed book, read the book's introductory material and the first page of the index. You may discover that certain sections—such as appendices, long lists of names, or material already arranged alphabetically—were not indexed. In such cases, you must examine these sections separately. Also, look up a few items in the text to see how complete the index is. Indexes in older books tend to be incomplete. Carefully examine the table of contents to see which chapters may be worth searching page by page. Fortunately, some old books are now being computerized in CD-ROM format, which makes every word in the book searchable.

Obtaining Information From Other Libraries

If you need a book that your local library does not have, you can use several methods to locate it. In public or university libraries, you can ask the librarian to obtain the desired book from another library. Interlibrary loan provides a good method for borrowing many titles; however, most libraries refuse to loan or photocopy rare or fragile books.

If there is an LDS family history center nearby (these centers are described later in this chapter in the section on the LDS Family History Library), go there and check the following sources: the *Microfiche Reference Collections*, which contains the full text of many published (mostly noncopyrighted) genealogical sources; and the *Family History Library Catalog* (FHLC), which describes the huge collections of the Family History Library. You can access most of the resources listed in the FHLC through a reasonably priced photocopy-by-mail service. To use this service, ask for photoduplication forms at the family history center.

See if your library has any editions of *Genealogical and Local History Books in Print*. The original editor of this classic work, Netti Schreiner-Yantis, added two supplements comprising some eight hundred pages' worth of genealogical titles by both subject and locality, to make earlier editions current through 1992. A new fifth edition is now being published, but this time in parts (reflecting the ever-increasing proliferation of genealogical works), by editor Marian R. Hoffman. The first part is a family history volume published in 1996 that lists over 4,600 available family histories.

Another helpful reference is Myers, Karns, and Henderson's *Genealogy from the Heartland. A Catalog of Titles in the Mid-Continent Public Library Genealogy Circulating Collection*, which is offered free to libraries. If your library offers an interlibrary loan service, you can borrow any of the three thousand genealogical books listed in this catalog.

Focusing Your Research

Knowing how to use catalogs, indexes, and other research tools will help you only to the extent that you are thorough in looking for names, locations, and any other topics relevant to your research. To ensure thoroughness, we suggest the following targeted approach: First, aim for the "bull's eye" (that is, a particular family in its specific location). For instance, if you are interested in the Cyrus Brown family residing in Hard Rock, Rye County, Kansas, the bull's-eye name and place are Cyrus Brown and Hard Rock, Kansas. If the card catalog gives no headings for Cyrus Brown or Hard Rock, you must expand the target by looking for any members of the Brown family in Rye County.

If you find no Browns in Rye County, enlarge your target again and check for Browns in surrounding counties and, if necessary, in the whole of Kansas. It shouldn't be too difficult to check a number of indexes for each known member of the Cyrus Brown family.

If you are still unsuccessful, try searching for related names, such as Funk (Cyrus' wife's maiden name), Showalter (his mother-in-law's maiden name), and Read (his daughter's husband's name). Any book or index entry pertaining to the Kansas Funks, Showalters, or Reads might also include clues for your Cyrus Brown investigation.

Expand your target whenever you learn of in-laws or suspected relatives, including neighbors of the same surname and names that appear in conjunction with your family name(s) in public or family records. For example, note witnesses or sponsors for your family's deeds, wills, or christenings, as well as plaintiffs and defendants in your family's court records. If several Humphreys are buried among your Browns in the Hard Rock town cemetery, include the name Humphrey in your research.

Developments in Library Research

Increasingly, libraries and information centers are automating their services. First, libraries acquired photocopy machines, then automated catalogs; now they are acquiring new services that include CD-ROM workstations and modems. In addition, many libraries use micropublishing—publishing books or collections of books or periodicals on microfilms and microfiche—to save space and money. Filming is generally done at large research libraries. Smaller libraries then buy these publications, so be sure to look for them during your library research.

Electronic Databases

Electronic databases offer substantial increases in speed and accuracy through techniques such as specific field searching, Boolean logic, and proximity operators. A manual search of New York City for a two-year time period would normally require you to sift through volumes of irrelevant data, but with a computer, you can tailor your search—for example, you could enter the key words, "New York City" and "not Irish," and the dates, "1850–1852," and the computer would search the appropriate databases quickly and efficiently.

Another advantage of searching electronic databases is the increased number of access points. When you look up the name Funk in a computerized *Who's Who*, in addition to the few notables indexed under that surname, you can find all additional Funks mentioned anywhere in the database—a spouse or mother with the maiden or middle name of Funk, an in-law Funk, a work-associate Funk, and so on. Electronic searching creates many more possibilities than are feasible in traditional research resources.

Increasing numbers of electronic genealogy databases are becoming available, including the following:

- **Bureau of Land Management database:** Recently opened, this database enables you to search for early land records of many eastern states. (See details in Chapter 7.)

- **Manuscript Society Information Exchange database:** This fee-based database, maintained by the Department of Archives and Manuscripts at Arizona State University, lists manuscripts, documents, and letters held by private individuals throughout the U.S. It enables researchers to access primary source materials held in private collections. These materials either are written by, about, or to famous individuals (Sam Houston, Davy Crockett, Aldous Huxley, Florence Nightingale, Virginia Woolf, Johannes Brahms, Giacomo Puccini, Mark Twain, and many others), or pertain to historical events (the Revolutionary and Civil Wars, the California gold rush, polar exploration, Indians of North America, colonial history, World War II, western Americana, and so on). You can obtain search forms and additional information by writing to Information Services, Archives and Manuscripts, Hayden Library, Arizona State University, Tempe, Arizona 85287-1006.

- **Library of Congress databases:** The Library of Congress, which contains the largest accumulation of knowledge in the world, has been producing historical collections in electronic form since 1990. These databases incorporate such difficult-to-locate items as pamphlets, photographs, and folklore. They also include life-history interviews conducted by the Depression-era WPA (Work Projects Administration) Folklore Project and published narratives of California's early years, dating back to 1849. By the year 2000, a core portion of the Library of Congress collections, including location information from online directories, will be accessible online.

Individual states and counties are also assembling databases of original court records. (Some of these developments are detailed in Chapter 7.)

The Internet

The most recent service offered by libraries is access to the Internet. Through some library workstations, you can access not only the Internet, but also a local database at the library or its online catalog. If you choose to use the Internet, your computer usually connects to a World Wide Web (WWW) browser, which is a hypertext interface that enables you to search internationally for text, full-color pictures, and sound bites, as well as the online catalogs of other libraries. Larger libraries offer commercial online services through their own WWW sites, which means that as long as you are using one of the library's computers, you can use the library's identification and password to quickly search electronic encyclopedias, full-text magazine articles, online indexes of articles, electronic telephone directories, and other materials that may require weeks or months of manual searching.

Some large European libraries are actively exploring new storage technologies; many materials important to your research will one day be retrievable over phone lines by libraries and home computers.

Online Public Access Catalogs (OPACs)

Most university and many public libraries, including the Library of Congress, have switched from card catalogs to computerized catalogs. Many of these catalogs are available online; they are known as Online Public Access Catalogs (OPACs).

Library OPACs aren't limited to the U.S.—all major research libraries in the United Kingdom have them. And through the Internet, you can find a book in Australia or Germany as easily as you can locate it in Cleveland or Detroit. A group in Bergen, Norway, regularly accesses a California library OPAC through the Internet because it is so much faster than accessing local library holdings! Using OPACs requires some basic technical knowledge, so beginning computer users should gain some familiarity with and confidence in using telecommunications technology before attempting remote catalog searches.

Of course, getting your hands on a genealogical book you find in an OPAC is more difficult than merely locating it, but perhaps not as difficult as you may think. In the vicinity of most large libraries, you can find businesses that will make photocopies from books and mail them to you for a fee. Many online sources (such as bulletin boards) allow you to ask questions to obtain details concerning specific research services.

A drawback to OPACs is that not all are complete. While libraries add all new acquisitions to their OPACs, the books held before they began automation may be added only gradually, or perhaps not at all. In such cases you must use traditional library-housed catalogs to learn about older genealogical books and journals. (For more information on OPACs and their use, see the cover article of *Genealogical Computing* in the April/May/June 1995 issue [number 14:4]. The author of the article, George Thurston, has included a partial listing of OPACs that contain relevant material for genealogists.)

CD-ROM Workstations

Many libraries now offer CD-ROM-equipped computers (often called CD-ROM workstations). CD-ROMs, described in Chapter 12, can improve the efficacy of searches by enabling you to quickly locate specific items within large amounts of data.

Popular CD-ROM products, which you can often find even in small libraries, are electronic telephone directories. One CD-ROM set can hold the information of hundreds of printed telephone books and can include similar information—so you can find all instances of the name you're looking for in a few seconds. Unfortunately, most of the current, inexpensive electronic white pages have been compiled from sources other than telephone directories, so their data is often incomplete and outdated. Nevertheless, these easy-to-find sources offer some value to genealogists now, and, like many software products, electronic telephone directories will improve in future versions. Other CD-ROM titles are provided in Chapter 12 of this book.

LDS Family History Library

Throughout this book we refer to LDS family history centers and to their mother source, the Family History Library (FHL). These facilities are operated by the Family History Department of The Church of Jesus Christ of Latter-day Saints (also known as the LDS or Mormon church).

The FHL is an important resource for all genealogists; it contains the world's largest and fastest-growing collection of genealogical records. Its location and name have changed several times since its founding in 1894, when it consisted of about one hundred volumes housed in a small room. Now occupying its own multi-level building, the FHL provides several daily tours and reference desks staffed by knowledgeable and friendly volunteers. (FHL address: 35 North West Temple Street, Salt Lake City, Utah 84150.)

One block east of the FHL is the recently renovated Joseph Smith Memorial Building, which contains a large room equipped with more than one hundred computers and printers for running the LDS church's Family Search software. Dozens of volunteers—who speak a variety of languages—are trained to teach people how to use this equipment. We highly recommend a visit to these almost-adjacent facilities if you ever visit Salt Lake City.

Family History Centers

Even if you never visit the FHL itself, you can utilize many of its collections through an international system of branch libraries known as family history centers. This system, which has been in place for many years, was established so that LDS church members living far from their church's headquarters (Salt Lake City, Utah) could access the information housed at the Family History Library. The LDS church has grown rapidly during the past quarter century and has used modern technology to sustain and support that growth. The branch library system has grown concurrently. Today there are more than 2,500 family history centers. Most are located in the U.S. and Canada, and many are fairly new. We expect many more (albeit smaller) centers to open at the local LDS congregation level and eventually to be available throughout the world.

Each family history center contains copies of several computerized genealogical collections accumulated and compiled by the LDS church. Family history centers also provide access, through loan, to the huge collection of microfilms housed in the Family History Library.

To obtain the address and hours of the family history center nearest you, contact the local Church of Jesus Christ of Latter-day Saints listed under "Churches" in the white or yellow pages of your telephone directory, or contact the FHL (see address above) to request a current listing of family history centers in your area. If you learn that the nearest family history center is some distance away, you can inform local LDS church leadership of your interest and willingness to help staff a local facility. The success of the family history centers rests upon the willingness of individuals to contribute their time and abilities. Many people who are not LDS church members have played an important part in making the family history center system successful.

Recent Work by the Family History Department

The accomplishments of the LDS Family History Department are impressive: It has microfilmed marriage, birth, christening, death, and burial records for millions of deceased people; coordinated large-scale volunteer efforts to organize many of these records into easy-to-search databases; enhanced the value of these databases through an efficient system of quality checks; and established an efficient and fast-growing library system for easy access to all of this data. Trained volunteers extract names from microfilmed original records. Then paired trained extractors use computerized techniques to produce large-scale databases with surprisingly few errors.

The Family History Department first issued these computerized databases on microfiche, which are 4"x 6" film-like cards, each containing thousands of indexed names with accompanying data. As computer technology has become less expensive, the Family History Department has issued several of the larger databases on CD-ROM.

Since 1939 the LDS church has used microfilming to copy original records. Most microfilms are duplicated and published in the *Family History Library Catalog* (FHLC). Updated twice yearly, the FHLC includes details on new acquisitions as soon as they become available to the public. As of early 1996, 1.9 million rolls of microfilm and 523,000 microfiche had been published in this worldwide effort. Of the microfilm rolls, 587,000 were for the U.S.; 35,000 were for Canada; 155,000 were for Great Britain; 585,000 were for Europe; 206,000 were for Scandinavia; and 205,000 were for Latin America. In 1993, more than 110 million pages of new material were filmed. Half of that material was for the U.S., the Philippines, and Great Britain. More than one million pages each were filmed in Italy, Spain, France, Canada, the Netherlands, Germany, Austria, Mexico, Sri Lanka, China, Sweden, Brazil, and Belgium. Additional filming took place in South Africa, Columbia, Indonesia, Hungary, Poland, Australia, Japan, Fiji, India, Switzerland, Peru, Jamaica, Ecuador, Guatemala, Puerto Rico, Greece, Portugal, Korea, Norway, Grenada, Yugoslavia, and the Leeward Islands. In the years following 1993, several countries with previously unobtainable records that had been locked behind the Iron Curtain have also begun to participate, including Bulgaria, Croatia, Estonia, Slovakia, Slovenia, and Russia.

FHL Collections and Computerized Databases

The FHL houses family histories, maps, references, and other compiled sources in some quarter-million bound volumes. It also contains a large manuscript collection of family histories. You can use a computerized catalog to access this wealth of material by place, surname, author, and subject. Even if a surname for which you are searching does not appear in a book's title, if the name appears prominently in the book, you can access that book by searching under the surname in the catalog. The equivalent of some six million published books of original records have been copied on microfilm. Most films are duplicated and made available for public use in both the FHL and family history centers.

Until 1989, the LDS computer databases were issued almost exclusively as microfiche collections. Since then, CD-ROM collections accessible through FamilySearch software have been issued. Some databases (including the International Genealogical Index [IGI], the FHLC, and Scottish Church Records) are available in both microfiche and CD-ROM format. Others are available only as CD-ROMs.

You can access the Family History Library's published and original microfilmed records at family history centers through the FHL's loan and photocopy services. In addition, family history centers usually have copies of the FHL's fiche and CD-ROM databases.

FamilySearch Software

An easy-to-learn software package called FamilySearch can help you search the FHL's CD-ROM collections. You can teach yourself to use FamilySearch by carefully reading and following the instructions that appear on each screen in the program. For indexed names in any collection, you use the up and down arrow keys to select the name you wish, then press Enter to display more detailed information. A bar at the top of each data screen lists additional options. Most family history centers require you to sign up for computer use and limit your computer time to one hour. Call in advance for the hours of operation and scheduling information.

You can find most FamilySearch CD-ROMs at family history centers and, of course, at the LDS Family History Library. Several nonprofit libraries and genealogical societies also carry the collections, and many LDS meetinghouses can now request and house the FamilySearch CD-ROM collections as well. All of these sites carry the IGI, Ancestral File, the Social Security and Military Death Indexes, and Scottish Church Records on CD-ROM.

In addition to the CD-ROM collections explained in this chapter, several other outstanding collections are now being compiled. The FamilySearch CD-ROMs are also being tested for home use; they may become available for individual purchase.

International Genealogical Index (IGI)

The IGI, available on either microfiche or CD-ROM, contains the names of deceased persons. About half of these names have been extracted from primary records (mostly parish registers), and the rest have been derived from LDS member-submitted temple work. A major extraction project of all early (pre-

1970) temple data was recently completed, and initial results of that project constitute the largest part of the 1994 Addendum to the IGI. At least one more addendum containing the remainder of the data will be forthcoming. However, the Family History Department does not verify this information, and because most of the LDS church members who submitted this data were amateur genealogists, you can expect more mistakes in this portion of IGI data. (On the other hand, information that individuals submit on their own families is generally quite accurate.)

Scope

Some 200 million names are indexed in the 1993 CD-ROM edition of the IGI—an increase of 13 million names from the 1992 microfiche edition. The 1994 Addendum to the IGI (consisting of a separate set of CD-ROMs published in July 1995) increased those numbers to 240 million; however, many of those names are duplicates. Most of the information extracted from parish registers is for people who lived between the early 1500s and 1885. Because name extraction began more than twenty-five years ago in England, the area and time period with the largest representation is seventeenth- through nineteenth-century England. Scandinavia and parts of Europe, such as Austria, Germany, and Switzerland, are also well-represented. The most complete U.S. coverage is for early New England. The IGI also contains many names from Mexico and the Philippines. Fewer names are included for other Latin American and Far Eastern countries, but the number is increasing.

These extracted entries are, of course, event-based (birth, christening, and marriage, for example). So if children are linked to their parents or if spouses are linked to each other in the original record, as is usually the case, those relationships appear in the IGI. For temple submission records, however, beginning with the 1992 edition, the name of another relative (often one who joined the LDS church) may appear instead of the spouse or parents' names (see Mr. Epes, Travis H. Epes, and Abigail Epes in Figure 4-1). In the microfiche edition, the # symbol appears by a name if parents are listed in a marriage record, or grandparents in a christening record. The "A" and "α" symbols indicate the appearance of other relatives' names in the original record. Except for these marks, nothing in the microfiche IGI links family members. The CD-ROM edition, on the other hand, groups possible brothers and sisters together; you can locate these groups through the database's "Parent Search" option.

If the batch number of a record begins with M (for Marriage) or C (for Christening), the piece of data was extracted from a primary record; this is true for the microfiche and CD-ROM versions, as well as the Addendum. Batch numbers consisting entirely of numbers indicate that the information was derived from LDS church member submissions. You can access further data source information through menus provided in FamilySearch software. The microfiche version requires you to use a separate fiche labeled "IGI Batch Number Index" to access source data; ask a library attendant to assist you or read the research guide *Finding an IGI Source* for details.

Setup and Use

Both microfiche and CD-ROM IGI data is clustered by geographic region, either in single countries or groups of countries (such as Continental Europe or Asia). Each region, in turn, is subdivided into smaller localities or subregions (countries, states, counties, parishes, and so on).

When you enter the IGI through FamilySearch, a window appears with a list of regions. You choose one to enter the database. If you don't know which region a certain country belongs in, you can use the country list in the window to help you identify the appropriate region. The list also includes a World Miscellaneous category, which may include names with mistyped locations or with incomplete location information.

The CD-ROM version includes greater searching capabilities than does the microfiche version. Using the CD-ROM, you can search an entire region at once, rather than searching separately in each subregion, as the microfiche requires. You can also limit your searches by place (country, state, or county), time period, or exact name spelling. When you find a name you are interested in, you can immediately switch to another part of the database to search for that individual's parents, siblings, or spouse.

Searching by Name

In several places (Denmark, Iceland, Finland, Norway, Sweden, Wales, and Monmouth County, England [now Gwent, Wales]), patronymic naming systems were used until relatively recently. Patronymic surnames generally change with each generation; the IGI allows you to search by given name as well as surname in these areas. Choose the Given Name option if you don't know the surname or can't find an individual under his or her surname.

In the microfiche edition, names within each subregion are listed alphabetically by last name, then by given name, then chronologically by event date. In both microfiche and CD-ROM editions, the event type is specified by a letter following the gender of the individual: B=birth, C=christening, D=death, M=marriage, N=census, and W=will or probate. The same person may be listed more than once if the name was extracted from more than one record or submitted multiple times (as, for example, for Mr. Epes and Amey Epes, the daughter of Edward and Mary, in Figure 4-1).

Also in the microfiche version, names extracted from original parish records are reproduced and listed alphabetically using the same spelling as the original; the spelling used in any given record may vary from the spelling you're familiar with. Alternative spellings of surnames are listed under a standard spelling (for example, "Eppert: see Eppard" in Figure 4-1). This usually simplifies your search, but not always; the standard surname may not be inclusive enough to cover every case. For example, the surname Gwynn includes the variants Gwin, Gwinn, Gwinne, Gwen, Guewin, Gwan, Gwynes, Gwyn, Gwynn, and Gwynne; however, the variants Gwyun and Gwywn are found under separate listings. In other examples, Bouyth is listed separately from Booth; Boutwright is not referenced under Boatwright; and Macklure is not listed as a variant of McClure. Such exceptions can trip all but the most savvy searcher. A surname phonetic standard (to replace the inadequate standard previously used) appears in the North American section of the 1993 IGI. While imperfect, this standard has already eliminated many alternative spelling omissions, such as those noted above.

Given names can cause as many problems as surnames. Under just one surname we checked, we found the following variants of Benjamin: Beniamin, Beniamine, Benianin, Beniman, Benj., Benja., Benjam., Benjamin, Benjamen, Benjm., Benjam., Benjaminus, Benjan., Benjani., Benjmin, Benjn., Bengamin, Bengemen, Bengemin, and Bengemon. Individuals with middle names or initials are listed after those without; for example, Hannah Elizabeth Jackson would follow all Hannah Jacksons. The IGI contains many misfilings regarding middle names, especially for the southern states, where surnames are commonly used as middle names. For example, in the 1992 version of the IGI, the false surname headings Armistead Edwards and Thruston Ball are shown for individuals whose middle names are Armistead and Thruston, rather than under the correct headings of Edwards and Ball. You may have to skip around frequently to find all possible candidates.

Fortunately, the 1993 CD-ROM version has begun to address such problems. It groups similarly spelled given names under a standard spelling, so whether a name is spelled Jhon, Johannes or Jno, and regardless of the presence of a middle name or initial, all are grouped chronologically under a standard spelling (in this case, John). This facilitates searching and increases your chances of finding the names you need. However, the system still is not perfect. Common nicknames (for example, Bill for William and Polly for Mary) are still grouped separately from the names to which they apply.

EPPERSON, WILLIA

COUNTRY UNITED STATES STATE: VIRGINIA AS OF MAR 1992 PAGE 10,115

NAME	FATHER / MOTHER OR SPOUSE OR RELATIVE (M=MALE F=FEMALE H=HUSBAND W=WIFE)		TYPE	EVENT DATE	COUNTY, TOWN, PARISH	B	E	S	SOURCE BATCH/FILM NO	SOURCE SERIAL SHEET
EPPERSON, WILLIAM										
EPPERSON, WILLIAM	POLLY PRIDDY	H	M	14OCT1806	HALIFAX			05SEP1973AZ	7230715	22
EPPERSON, WILLIAM	NANCY CLAY	H	M	25JUN1808	HALIFAX			05SEP1973AZ	7230715	21
EPPERSON, WILLIAM	NANCY CLAY	H	M	26JUN1808	HALIFAX			06MAR1959SL	A457423	1073
EPPERSON, WILLIAM ə	WILLIAM EPPERSON/NANCY	M	B	1817	PATRICK CO.	05JAN1955IF	16FEB1956IF	PRE-1970	0442351	FILM
EPPERSON, WILLIAM	SAMUEL R. EPPERSON/SARAH TUCKER	M	B	1842	HALIFAX	13JAN1990AT	18JAN1990AT	19JAN1990AT	5010746	31
EPPERSON, WILLIAM ə	RELATIVE: ARNOLD E. RIDGWAY/	M	B	ABT. 1846	HALLIFAX CO.	11APR1916SL	PRE-1970	PRE-1970	0183465	FILM
EPPERSON, WILLIAM	FRANCES BROWN	H	M	12NOV1846	WYTHE			20MAY1988PV	8728804	42
APPERSON, WILLIAM CUMBERLAND		M	B	19OCT1833	CULPEPER	22APR1989JA	12MAY1989WA		8904501	1
EPPERSON, WILLIAM D.	GEORGIA E. S. WILLIAM	H	M	24DEC1883	BRUNSWICK			17DEC1981SL	8111306	26
EPPERSON, WILLIAM H.	MARY N. DULANEY	H	M	13JUN1844	SCOTT			30APR1974PV	7324218	91
EPPERSON, WILLIAM J. ə	WILLIAM EPPERSON/MARY POLLY EPPERSON	M	B	1847	PATRICK CO.	05JAN1955IF	16FEB1956IF	PRE-1970	0442651	FILM
HEFERSON, WILLIAM M.	ELIZABETH JONES	H	M	14OCT1830	CUMBERLAND			26JAN1983JR	8111909	19
EPPERSON, WILLIAM R.	ELIZABETH FOREST	H	M	11JUN1830	HALIFAX			30NOV1955SL	A457007	0435
EPPERSON, WILLIAM RICHARD THOMAS ə	RELATIVE: RALEIGH L. MATHENA JR./	M	B	09FEB1869	TAZEWELL CO., OF BAILEY	29MAY1943AZ	PRE-1970	PRE-1970	0170633	FILM
APPERSON, WM. C.	MARTHA FRANCES GLASSCOCK	H	M	1857	CULPEPER	22APR1955	18JUN1957SL	01APR1958SL	C504901	1098
EPPERSON, [illegible]UNG YOUNG	MARTHA AUSTIN	H	M	08FEB1828	WASHINGTON			30JAN1992OG	1760800	FILM
EPPERSSON								28JAN1957SL	A457118	1682
EPPERSSON, MRS. ELIZABETH ə	RELATIVE: SIDNEY HYRUM EPPERSON/	F	B	1307	OF NEW KENT CO.	12MAY1938SL	PRE-1970	PRE-1970	0183574	FILM
EPPERSSON, JUDITH ə	RELATIVE: SIDNEY HYRUM EPPERSON/	F	B	1768	ALBEMARLE CO.	12MAY1938SL	PRE-1970	PRE-1970	0183574	FILM
EPPERT, •• SEE EPPARD										
EPPES •• SEE ALSO ••										
•• APEY	•• EPEY									
•• EPP	•• HAPPEY									
•• IPE										
EPPS, MR.	MRS. ELIZABETH EPPS	H	M	1673	WILLIAMSBURG			17JAN1992MT	1760778	FILM
EPPS, MR.	MRS. ELIZABETH EPPS	H	M	1673	WILLIAMSBURG			22JAN1992MT	1760783	FILM
EPPS, MR. ə	RELATIVE: FREDERICK W. COX/	M	B	ABT. 1711	HENRICO, OF BREMO	22MAR1927MT	PRE-1970	PRE-1970	0170410	FILM
EPES, (COL.) TRAVIS H. ə	RELATIVE: DANIEL WEBSTER JONES/	M	B	ABT. 1810	OF AMELIA CO.	26JAN1935AZ	PRE-1970	PRE-1970	0170628	FILM
EPPES, ABIGAIL ə	RELATIVE: JESSE KNIGHT/	F	B	ABT. 1724		01MAR1910SL	PRE-1970	PRE-1970	0183444	FILM
EPPES, AMEY Δə	SPOUSE: WILLIAM WORSHAM/	F	S	ABT. 1717	CHESTERFIELD,,OF	30APR1990JR	06JUN1990JR		F515401	0012
EPPES, AMEY Δə	WILLIAM WORSHAM	W	M	‹1736›	CHESTERFIELD			03MAY1990JR	F515401	0012
EPPES, AMY	EDWARD EPPES/MARY ANDERSON	F	B	19SEP1739	SURRY	CHILD	CHILD	27OCT1988SE	5004937	24
EPS, AMY	EDWARD EPS/MARY	F	C	20NOV1739	SURRY, ALBEMARLE PARISH	03MAR1976SL	24APR1976SL	15JUN1976SL	C504641	0002
EPPES, AMY	EDWARD EPPES/MARY ANDERSON	F	C	30NOV1739	ALBEMARLE, ST ANNE'S PARISH					
EPES, AMY	CHARLES CLAY	W	M	09JUN1804	AMELIA	CHILD	CHILD	10NOV1977OK	7704709	17
EPPES, ANGELICA ə	RELATIVE: WILLIAM J. BENNETT/	F	B	ABT. 1722	CHARLES CITY CO.	21SEP1943AL	PRE-1970	08SEP1989OG / PRE-1970	8901107 / 0170768	41 / FILM
EPPES, ANN ə	RELATIVE: WILLIAM J. BENNETT/	F	B	ABT. 1718	CHARLES CITY CO.	21SEP1943AL	PRE-1970	PRE-1970	0170768	FILM
EPPES, ANN	EDWARD EPPES/MARY ANDERSON	F	B	15SEP1743	SURRY	02NOV1935	01MAY1936AZ	16MAR1954SL	5004937	24

Δ= ENTRY ALTERED FROM SOURCE; ə,ə,›=RELATIVES NAMED IN SOURCE. SEE "SYMBOLS" IN INSTRUCTIONS.

A = ADULT CHRISTENING B = BIRTH C = CHRISTENING D = DEATH OR BURIAL ALL OTHERS = MISCELLANEOUS
F = BIRTH OR CHRISTENING OF FIRST KNOWN CHILD M = MARRIAGE N = CENSUS W = WILL

Figure 4-1. IGI Extract

Printing and Copying to Diskette

With the CD-ROM version of the IGI, you can copy data to a diskette or print it out on paper. Copying to a diskette is much faster than printing and saves money and paper. Before you print or copy to a diskette, use the Holding File option to save hundreds of entries to one file.

When you copy to a diskette, you can save data as either GEDCOM or ASCII files. If you save data in ASCII format, you can file it in your word processor, protect your database from corruption by inaccurate data, and maintain easy access to the material. On the other hand, some software (including Personal Ancestral File, or PAF) allows you to keep separate GEDCOM files, so you can compare your IGI GEDCOM data with the individual records in your database (and merge them, if you desire). This gives you flexibility to incorporate any helpful data you find without contaminating your database with suspect information.

Ancestral File

Ancestral File has been several years in the making. It began in the 1970s, when LDS church members were encouraged to submit pedigrees and family group charts on their ancestors. The Family History Department spent several years converting this information into electronic form. After its publication in 1991, Ancestral File was made available to the public. Today, submissions are accepted from all researchers.

Scope, Submissions, and Corrections

Ancestral File is the world's most extensive resource for helping you learn about and contact others who are interested in the same family lines as you are. Ancestral File, updated and published every year or two, has grown rapidly, albeit sporadically. The second edition was forty percent larger than the original; the third about thirty percent larger than the second. The fourth edition is not much larger than the third—it contains only 15 million pedigree-linked names and includes no contributions past August 1992. However, extensive revisions to various compression techniques improved the software's performance and speed. The fifth edition, expected to be released in early 1997, will be nearly twice the size of the fourth. Thereafter, future editions are expected to appear on a more frequent basis.

If you can't locate information on a family line in the current Ancestral File, or if you find that you already have more information than is in the Ancestral File, you can request the brochure "Contributing Information to the Ancestral File" from a family history center or the Ancestral File Operations Unit of the Family History Library. This brochure explains how to submit computerized data, including additions. The Family History Department still accepts (albeit reluctantly) data submitted on paper, as well. However, this method introduces the possibility of error as your data is entered by volunteers. In addition, paper submissions can take as much as a year longer to process than computer-produced GEDCOM file submissions. The Ancestral File Operations Unit routinely sends postcards to confirm its receipt of your data; if you don't receive one within six weeks of submission, contact the unit at 1-801-240-4874.

Most of the data in Ancestral File (including LDS temple dates) was submitted by amateur researchers and is not always current or accurate. While the Family History Department does not review this data, it does allow users to make corrections. If you use Ancestral File, you can make corrections as you discover mistakes. Although you should not resubmit names already in the database, if you spot incorrect information, you can learn how to correct it by obtaining an instruction sheet called "Correcting Information in Ancestral File," available at any family history center.

Only the most recent corrections are included in any edition, so you should coordinate your efforts with those of others working on the same line. The name and address of each person who makes corrections, along with reasons and/or sources for those corrections, are saved in each file's History of Changes section. You can contact researchers who have submitted or changed information for any individual in the file. (This feature of Ancestral File replaces and improves upon the Family Registry, a microfiche collection begun in late 1983. It grew to include more than 300,000 active researchers until it was phased out in early 1994.)

Formats
FamilySearch software enables you to view and print Ancestral File data in the following formats:

1. Alphabetized index

2. Numerical index (each name is assigned a unique number by which it can be accessed)

3. Pedigree charts

4. Descendant charts

5. Family Group charts on which the individual is listed as a parent

6. Family Group charts on which the individual is listed as a child

You may not find all names in all formats. Name-Only records do not contain all the facts that you'll find on Individual records, which contain data concerning birth, death, parents, marriage, LDS ordinances, names and addresses of submitters, notes, and histories of file changes. Some Name-Only records, in fact, show only the designation "Living," with or without a name. These records contain data for persons born during the last 110 years, submitted without a death date (so an individual designated "Living" may not be alive still).

Printouts can be surprisingly long: A Descendant chart can show as many as five generations of descendants, which may number in the thousands; and Pedigree charts list all known ancestors for all lines.

Storing Finished Research

As volunteers in a family history center, we often hear first-time users ask, "How much do we owe you?" Many are amazed to learn that most services are free. (Exceptions include printouts, photocopies, and postage for microfilm orders.) Rather than seeking financial assistance, the Family History Department requests participation; specifically, the department asks you to submit the results of your research to the FHL collections so that these results can be shared with others.

This attitude is commendable. Some of the worst scenarios for family researchers occur when they make no provision to preserve their research. Family members who survive researchers often do not know what to do with the information, so in many cases it is lost or destroyed. Sharing research by submitting it to Ancestral File not only protects data from possible catastrophes (fire, flood, war, and so on) and the inevitable death of the researcher, it also kindles interest and aids others in their research.

When you contribute your research to Ancestral File, you can be sure it will not be lost or discarded. However, you should list sources for all data so that your findings are credible and won't be "corrected" by someone whose sources may not be as reliable as yours.

Scottish Church Records on CD-ROM

The *Index to the Old Parochial Registers of Scotland*, originally issued on microfiche in 1991, is a boon if you are researching Scottish ancestry. It includes all surviving legible marriage and christening records in that country's 901 Church of Scotland (Presbyterian) parishes and associated Kirk Session records up to the year 1855, when Civil Registration began. These records were carefully extracted and indexed into files for each Scottish county. Names are listed in both a surname and given-name index.

Damaged pages and blotted, faded, or otherwise illegible names, which might normally be overlooked or inaccurately transcribed, are often indexed in different ways than you might expect. The beginning of the microfiche collection contains instructions (which you can also obtain in hard copy) for researching such cases. Although these instructions are somewhat tedious, they can help you locate names that might be impossible to find otherwise. All the data contained in the *Index to the Old Parochial Registers of Scotland,* as well as several thousand additional non-conformist records (about ten million names in all), has been published recently on a CD-ROM entitled *Scottish Church Records.* Using this CD-ROM simplifies your search and makes it possible to locate a name even if you don't know an individual's county of residence. In 1996, the CD-ROM became part of the FamilySearch software collection.

The Social Security and Military Death Indexes

Two other CD-ROM collections are included with FamilySearch: The Social Security Death Index and the Military Death Index. The Social Security Death Index is updated yearly and currently contains data for some 51 million people who registered with the Social Security Administration and died between 1962 and 1995. (A smattering of names predate 1962.) Information includes name, reported birth year, state that issued the social security number, state and year of death, and social security number. The index also includes a ZIP code directory, which can find an individual's place of death, and a vital records address register, which lists, state-by-state, addresses you can contact to obtain death certificates.

The Military Death Index contains data for almost 100,000 U.S. soldiers who died in the Vietnam and Korean Wars. More details are available for Vietnam than Korea, but all records include at least birth and death dates, death place, U.S. residence, rank, and service number.

Miscellaneous Collections

Microfilm collections vary in size and variety between family history centers, but even small ones often keep a number of microfilmed records relating to their local area. You can use the microfilmed census and/or vital records for at least the portion of the state that your family history center serves.

Microfiche and hard copy collections are more standardized among family history centers. You should be able to find the following resources at almost all family history centers:

Accelerated Indexing Systems (AIS) Census Indexes
Accelerated Indexes, a private firm, was the first organization to computerize and index the early U.S. censuses on a large scale. The LDS Family History

Department purchased the rights to the AIS microfiche indexes, which were compiled several years ago. Other computerized census indexes have since been published, some supposedly more accurate and complete. Nonetheless, with its scope of 37 million names, most between the years 1790 and 1850, the AIS collection is a good preliminary search tool.

PERiodical Source Index (PERSI)

The *PERiodical Source Index* (PERSI) on microfiche is licensed by the Allen County Public Library (in Fort Wayne, Indiana), which publishes the hard copy version. It is actually two separate indexes to genealogical magazines and journals: The recently completed 1847-1985 Index covers periodicals published during that time; a supplemental Annual Index (released yearly) covers virtually all genealogy magazines published since 1986. Nearly all English-language and French-Canadian genealogical periodicals have been, or will be, included in PERSI. While it is not as complete or detailed as some locally produced indexes, its scope enables rapid access to some half-million articles by locality, surname, or research "how-to's." To become more familiar with PERSI, ask a family history center librarian for the *PERSI Resource Guide*; instructions vary somewhat for each section.

Microfiche Reference Collections

A two-part microfiche collection of reference books, totalling some 225 published resources, is available at family history centers in the U.S. and Canada. Sources cover a considerable range and include some important early European gazetteers, several "how-to" texts, and a variety of compiled sources.

Printed Research Aids

Research outlines have been available from the FHL for several years, but in 1988 the Family History Department revised and standardized them. They can help you take full advantage of the materials in the extensive LDS collections. Research outlines are especially good for describing the resources available through the FHL. In addition, they are current, inexpensive, and thorough in their coverage of a variety of sources. You can obtain research outlines for many countries and each state in the U.S.; if an outline for a particular area has not yet been published when you first inquire, check back periodically. After examining relevant outlines, you may photocopy sections that interest you or purchase the entire outline. State research outlines cost 25 cents; country outlines are usually 75 cents.

An adjunct resource is the collection of word lists written to help English-speaking researchers with non-English materials. The lists are indexed by language name and include the English translations of words commonly found in genealogical records. If you are tracing early New York Dutch immigrant ancestors, for instance, the research outlines for New York and the Netherlands, as well as the word list for Dutch, would be helpful.

Catalogs and Loan System

The *Family History Library Catalog* (FHLC) may become your most valuable tool after you have exhausted family resources because it can help you locate and access the records in which your ancestors are most likely to appear. The FHLC is available on both microfiche and CD-ROM. With the CD-ROM version, you can download relevant catalog entries to your own diskette. The catalog consists of the following sections:

- **Surname catalog:** The Surname catalog is an index of the principal surnames found in the Family History Library's collection of genealogical books. This catalog can be especially helpful if you're researching common surnames. Its index may have thousands of entries for books containing information on a specific family name, but by adding additional names to a search (for example, Cyrus and Kansas), you can easily and quickly locate any entries relevant to your research.

- **Author-Title and Topical Subject catalogs:** The Author-Title and Topical Subject catalogs, which are available on microfiche only, allow you to find items through the author, title, and subject headings traditionally used in library collections.

- **Locality catalog:** Because it lists records by geographical name, the Locality catalog can provide an especially helpful way to access genealogical information. In the microfiche copy, place names are listed alphabetically following the next-larger jurisdiction. For instance, records from the town of Downey in Cedar County, Iowa, are listed after all Cedar County records and all Clarence town records but before all Tipton town records. (If the Downey town records are sparse, expand your search to include Cedar County and Iowa state record resources. Also, note that federal censuses are listed at the national level.)

With the computerized catalog, you can go directly to the geographical name of a small jurisdiction, even if you don't know its precise location. Suppose you know that an ancestor lived in the town of Downey—you believe the town is in Iowa. If you enter "Downey" in the appropriate field on the screen, a list will appear displaying every Downey in the world that the FHLC has records for; you can then determine which one is correct.

In both the microfiche and computerized copy, various kinds of records for any given locality are listed alphabetically by subject type—Census, Church, Map, Probate, and so on. Refer to the list of subject headings at the end of this chapter for some headings that may be useful in narrowing your searches.

If your research involves records in China, Japan, or Korea, you can use a separate Asian Microfilm Card Catalog, which is not directly accessible through the FHLC. Printed instructions are available for the catalog; you can obtain more information by contacting a family history center librarian.

Pending Collections

An excellent index of the 1881 census of England, Wales, the Channel Islands, and the Isle of Man was recently completed, thanks to the efforts of several thousand volunteers. It contains approximately 40 million names. Microfiche copies are already available in some areas, and a CD-ROM version is also expected. Also, an index to the 1880 U.S. census is being compiled and may be published before the end of the decade.

Name extraction has increased considerably in recent years. Many Family History Department projects are entered in the Genealogical Projects Registry database, which is maintained by the National Genealogical Society with the Family History Department. Societies and individuals engaged in genealogical projects should consult this register, then list their projects in it. Some projects conducted by the LDS Family History Department result in stand-alone collections, others become part of the FamilySearch collections, and still others are published in cooperation with governmental and/or volunteer groups (as explained in Chapter 12).

Bibliography

Library Genealogical Bibliographies

Cavanaugh, Karen B. *A Genealogist's Guide to the Fort Wayne, Indiana, Public Library*. 4th ed. Fort Wayne, IN: Watermill Publications, 1988.

Hamer, Collin B., Jr. *Genealogical Materials in the New Orleans Public Library*. New Orleans, LA: Friends of the New Orleans Public Library, 1984.

Hoffman, Marian R., ed. and comp. *Genealogical and Local History Books in Print: Family History Volume*. 5th ed. Baltimore: Genealogical Publishing Co., 1996.

Jaccaud, Robert D. *Passages to Family History. A Guide to Genealogical Research in the Dartmouth College Library*. Hanover, NH: Dartmouth College Library, 1990.

Nichols, Elizabeth L. *Genealogy in the Computer Age: Understanding FamilySearch*. Rev. ed. Salt Lake City, UT: Family History Educators, 1994. To order, write to P.O. Box 510606, Salt Lake City, UT 84151-0606.

Oldenburg, Joseph. *A Genealogical Guide to the Burton Historical Collection Detroit Public Library*. Salt Lake City, UT: Ancestry, 1988.

Parker, J. Carlyle. *Going to Salt Lake City to Do Family History Research*. 2nd ed., rev. and enl. Turlock, CA: Marietta Publishing Co., 1993.

Schreiner-Yantis, Netti. *Genealogical and Local History Books in Print*. 4th ed. Springfield, VA: Schreiner-Yantis, 1985. *Supplement* 1991.

Sinko, Peggy Tuck. *Guide to Local and Family History at the Newberry Library*. Salt Lake City, UT: Ancestry, 1987.

Subject Heading Checklist

Use the following subject headings to simplify your library research. Check these headings when using collections and catalogs. (LC = Library of Congress; FHL = Family History Library.)

Archive Collections
Atlases
Bible Records: See Vital Records (FHL); Family Records (LC)
Bibliographies
Biography
Birth Records: See Vital Records
Cemeteries: See Vital Records (FHL)
Census Schedules: See Census
Church History
Church Membership and Minutes: See Church Records (FHL); Church
    Records and Registers (LC)
City Directories: See Directories
City Histories: See History
Civil Records: See Court Records (LC)
County Histories: See History
County Atlases
Criminal Court Records: See Court Records
Death Records: See Vital Records
Emigration Records
Family Histories: locate under the surname
Gazetteers
Genealogy
Geographical Names: See Names, Geographical
Ghost Towns: See History, Geography (FHL); Cities & Towns, Ruined,
    Extinct, etc. (LC)
Historical Atlases: See Atlases (FHL); Historical Geography, Maps (LC)
Historical Societies: See Societies
Immigration Records
Land Ownership Maps
Land Records: See Land and Property (FHL); Deeds, Land Titles (LC)
Maps
Marriage Records: See Vital Records (FHL); Marriage Licenses (LC)
Military History: See Military Records (FHL); History, Military;
    Regimental Histories; History—Registers, Lists, etc.; Registers of Dead
    (LC)
Minorities
Mortality Schedules: See Vital Records (FHL); Genealogy—Sources;
    Census, (year); Mortality (LC)

Mortuary Records: See Vital Records (FHL); Mortality (LC)
Naturalization: See Emigration and Immigration (FHL)
Newspapers
Oral History
Patriotic Societies: See Societies (FHL)
Periodicals
Place Names: See Geographical Names
Plot Book: See Land & Property—Maps (FHL); Real Property—Maps (LC)
Poll Tax Lists: See Electorate (FHL); Poll—Tax (LC)
Post Offices: See Postal Guides (FHL); Postal Service (LC)
Probates: See Probate Records
Public Land: See Land and Property (FHL)
School Records: See Schools
Ship Passenger Lists: See Emigration and Immigration
Surnames: See Names, Personal
Tax Records: See Taxation
Vital Records: See Register of Births, etc. (LC)
Voter Lists: See Electorate (FHL); Voting Registers (LC)
Wills: See Probates

Chapter 5

Compiled Sources, Societies, and Periodicals

Compiled sources are books and databases that result from others' research. They generally contain abundant data, which may provide clues, if not a good basis, for your research. Of course, all compiled sources are likely to include some typographical errors at the least. Compiled sources are always considered secondary sources, which aren't as reliable as primary sources. (See Chapter 3 for an explanation of primary and secondary evidence.)

A compiled source can be valuable if the compiler used original records and if the work is accurate. It can be even more valuable if the work is also comprehensive, meaning that it covers most or all available relevant sources. Compiled sources vary in the degree to which they fulfill these criteria.

Ideally, you'll be able to find a compilation published by a meticulous, experienced researcher who carefully examined all pertinent sources for your family. Realistically, however, while a number of such works have appeared in recent years, they are still relatively rare. Nevertheless, even a work based on poorly compiled and inadequately documented research can still be a valuable resource. Perhaps, for example, its compiler had access to sources that are now lost, or talked with people who are now deceased.

Genealogies and Family Histories

You should search genealogies and family histories not only to prevent duplication of research, but also to gather helpful information on direct and related lines. Unfortunately, many genealogies and family histories have been written by naive, even careless researchers. The idea that genealogy should involve the same painstaking care for accuracy and documentation as other fields of scholarship is a notion that, unfortunately, has yet to take strong hold. Additionally, the author may not have had access to excellent historical sources that have only recently become generally available.

You should be skeptical of unsupported reports of famous ancestors who lived long ago. Pay special notice, however, to facts about family members who lived during that time—generally, the closer the time and relationship, the more reliable the evidence. Parker's *Library Services for Genealogists* contains a good list of published histories (pages 243-51).

Some fine genealogies and family histories exist for foreign research. Germany provides an excellent example with its many published and unpublished *Ortssippenbucher* (local clan books), compiled in the 1930s by local genealogists using card-cataloged vital entries from the German parish registers dating as far back as the 1600s, and local register offices for the 1875-1930 era. These books generally conform to high standards of accuracy—demographers and other scholars have used them for modern computerized studies. More than one hundred *Ortssippenbucher* have been published since 1937. To learn whether one exists for a particular community, write to the mayor or local minister.

Biographical Works

Look for biographies even if you are unaware of famous people in your ancestry—an ancestor in a family line that you're not familiar with may have been considered worthy of biographical mention.

Herbert and McNeil's *Biography and Genealogy Master Index*, available in both print and CD-ROM versions, is a popular reference that indexes more than 8.5 million biographies. It does not include local sources.

Slocum's *Biographical Dictionaries and Related Works* lists some 16,000 national, regional, state, and vocational publications.

County or town histories often include biographies. No nationwide source indexes all of them, but you can search state or local resources, such as the *Index to Biographies in Local Histories,* which identifies more than a quarter-million such biographies. Another book, Filby's *A Bibliography of American County Histories*, identifies five thousand county histories, many of which contain biographies. An excellent biographical source that serves as an example of what is available on a state level is Powell's *Dictionary of North Carolina Biography*.

Parker's *Going to Salt Lake City to Do Family History Research* contains two chapters—"Is There a Biographical Sketch About Your Ancestor?" and "Is an Ancestor's Name in National or Regional Indexes?"—that may help you locate pertinent biographies.

Local Histories, Registers, and Directories

In addition to providing historical and geographical background, local histories of towns, counties, and regions may contain biographical information. As with other types of compiled sources, you should use good judgment to evaluate their accuracy. Because many are old and contain information taken from the reports of contemporary informants, reading them can be somewhat like interviewing people who lived generations ago.

Other potentially valuable references include registers, directories, and comparable works for different states, organizations (such as the U.S. Army), and groups (such as early New England settlers). Because these compilations are normally created by experienced compilers using original records, they are often more accurate than other compiled sources.

Genealogical Societies and Periodicals

Local genealogical and historical societies and their associated periodicals and local history collections can be very good research sources. There are several thousand societies in the U.S. and Canada alone. Many research findings are published under their auspices in periodicals that may also include updates on additional compilations and indexes for the area.

Consider joining a society or subscribing to a magazine that caters to your genealogical interests. Many of these publications let readers publish free queries, which can be fruitful. If you have a chance to visit the area in which your ancestors lived, be sure to seek out local historical collections.

One purpose of local societies is to help people conducting genealogical research in their area. Affiliation gives you the opportunity to meet researchers who are knowledgeable and experienced in your area of interest. They can help when you become stuck in your research or don't know how to interpret a finding. Societies also typically sponsor conferences or seminars. Some societies sponsor online bulletin board systems (BBSs). One well-organized and popular BBS is run as a FidoNet node by the Texas State Genealogical Society; members of that society can read its journal online.

The Genealogical Helper is a good source of information on newly published genealogical works for all areas. During the past few years, the publisher has gathered family data from readers and published the information on a CD-ROM, which is available directly from their company, from Brøderbund, or from any of many other distributors who sell the Family Archives CDs (see Chapter 12). Some 930,000 ancestral names are included, though that number includes many duplicates.

Another national periodical is the *FGS Forum,* published by the Federation of Genealogical Societies. This high-quality publication helps network societies and individual subscribers. For details, write to a local society leader or the FGS (P.O. Box 830220, Richardson, TX 75083).

Hundreds of other genealogical publications, many of them practically unknown outside their small memberships, are published by family organizations or small local societies. They usually lack indexes, but various sources help to remedy this problem by indexing much of this important information. One outstanding and readily available resource is the *PERiodical Source Index* (PERSI) microfiche collection, described in Chapter 4, which indexes thousands of genealogical and historical magazines dating from 1847 to the present. Two other helpful indexes, *Genealogical Periodical Annual Index* and Jacobus' *Index to Genealogical Periodicals* are available in most large research libraries.

In the U.S., *The New England Historic Genealogical Register* and the *National Genealogical Society Quarterly* are well-known journals with articles that consistently exemplify high standards of accuracy in research. The New England Historic Genealogical Society has compiled all of its early registers, along with an index, in a nine-volume CD-ROM disk set that sells for $300 (including shipping) and can be ordered from their sales catalog web site: http://www.channel1.com/users/nehgs/salescat.htm. Many helpful periodicals are also published abroad: The *Federation of Family History Societies* in the United Kingdom is a good source for information on worldwide organizations and their affiliated journals.

In our extensive Virginia research, we have been helped by magazine indexes. Several important early genealogical magazines for Virginia are indexed in Swem's *Virginia Historical Index. The Virginia Genealogist* is a fine journal that has published two indexes covering its first thirty-five years, as well as a CD-ROM that includes graphic representations (as does the just-mentioned NEHGR set) of its first twenty volumes and of its index, and sells for $140. Many genealogical newsletters and journals likewise publish cumulative indexes; look for those covering your area of interest. (The *Genealogical Helper* lists current genealogical journals by geographical area each year.)

Newspapers

Newspaper collections for your ancestors' localities are a valuable resource. Some are indexed, and many are available on microfiche or microfilm. Ask your librarian about newspaper collections; you may be able to order them through interlibrary loan (see Chapter 4). The collections published on CD-ROM are certainly the easiest to research; we hope that many more will soon be available.

Secondary Evidence

Newspapers may be the only remaining source for certain facts. Obituary notices are a good example; others include birth, engagement, and marriage announcements; news items; or even advertisements. Below, we've abstracted some examples of secondary evidence from newspaper files. The following excerpts are from the *Virginia Gazette* and taken from Headley's *18th-Century Virginia Newspapers*:

Mrs. Mary Wynn of Greensville Co., [Va.] died in or about Oct. 1789. The said Mary gave to her sons, John and Robert Powell, a parcel of Negroes. Capt Manson of York Co., [Va.], claims some of the Negroes and Michael Malone of Sussex Co., [Va.] also claims them according to an advertisement by James Powell, executor of John Powell who was executor of Mary Wynn deceased and Mathew Davis, executor of Robert Powell. (28 Apr 1797)

John Bailey, apprentice boy, ran away from Thomas Roberts of Nansemond Co. [Va.] who suspects he is lurking about Hampton as he was born there. (24 Jun 1777)

Marcus Gibbin, youngest son of the Rev. John Gibbin of King's Co., Ireland, came to the back settlements in Philadelphia about 25 years ago and was a schoolmaster; if he be living, he is requested to write to Mrs. Martha Gibbin, Stephen St, Dublin. For further details, enquire of Marcus Gibbin of Chesterfield Co., [Va.]. (16 Jun 1774)

Genealogy Columns

Newspapers may include genealogy columns. For example, the *Boston Transcript* compiled great amounts of data throughout the nineteenth century. It has since been indexed and microfilmed and is available through the LDS Family History Library (see Chapter 4) and elsewhere. Many current newspapers carry valuable genealogy columns. A good source for locating them is Milner's *Newspaper Genealogical Columns Directory*.

If you find a genealogy column in a newspaper for the area you are researching, consider sending them a query about the family you are researching. It may attract the attention of a distant relative still living in your ancestral location or a local genealogist who is likely to read such columns.

Bibliography

Filby, P. William. *A Bibliography of American County Histories.* Baltimore, MD: Genealogical Publishing Co., 1985. Identifies five thousand county histories, many of which contain biographies.

Headley, Robert K., Jr. *18th-Century Virginia Newspapers.* Baltimore, MD: Genealogical Publishing Co., 1987.

Herbert, M.C., and B. McNeil. *Biography and Genealogy Master Index.* 8 vols. Detroit, MI: Gale Research Co., 1980, 1985-present. Five volumes and annual supplements since 1985.

Index to Biographies in Local Histories. Baltimore, MD: Magna Carta Book Co., 1979. Identifies more than a quarter-million biographies.

Jacobus, Donald L. *Index to Genealogical Periodicals 1932-1953.* Reprint. Baltimore, MD: Genealogical Publishing Co., 1973.

Milner, Anita Cheek. *Newspaper Genealogical Columns Directory.* 5th ed. Bowie, MD: Heritage Books, 1992.

Parker, J. Carlyle, ed. *Library Service for Genealogists.* Detroit, MI: Gale Research Co., 1981. Identifies the best published references (through the 1970s) for genealogists.

Parker, J. Carlyle. *Going to Salt Lake City to Do Family History Research.* 2nd ed. Turlock, CA: Marietta Publishing Co., 1993.

Powell, William S. *Dictionary of North Carolina Biography.* 6 vols. Chapel Hill, NC: University of North Carolina Press, 1979-96.

Slocum, Robert B., ed. *Biographical Dictionaries and Related Works.* 2nd ed. 2 vols. Detroit, MI: Gale Research Co., 1986.

Swem, Earl Le G., comp. *Virginia Historical Index.* Roanoke, VA: Stone Printing, 1934-1936. Reprint. Northampton, MS: Peter Smith, 1965. 2 vols. Name, place, subject index to important Virginia periodicals and compiled sources, through 1930.

The Genealogical Helper. Logan, UT: Everton Publishers. Publisher address: P.O. Box 368, Logan, UT 84321.

Chapter 6

Vital Records: Government, Church, and Cemetery

Vital records are those made at the time of a person's birth, marriage, and death. They may also include records of closely associated events. Christening, for example, usually takes place soon after a child's birth. Burial records, proclamations of intended marriage, and marriage bonds are usually prepared within a few days or weeks of death or marriage. (Note that engagement announcements and marriage bonds provide only circumstantial evidence of marriage, unless the marriage date was initialed afterward.)

Vital facts may have been recorded by any of several jurisdictions. Family records are the most common source of vital statistics. The other principal sources are government, church, and cemetery records.

Government Records

In the United States, vital records are of relatively recent origin, and therefore are weak in comparison with those of many other countries. Nevertheless, they can be helpful, and you should seek them after thoroughly examining family sources and before looking for any other records.

The state is the first jurisdiction to check for vital registration in the United States. Table 6-1 shows when each state initiated vital registration, or when most records start. In some cases, registration began earlier than the date listed for at least one large city within a state; for example, New Orleans began keeping birth records in 1790, but Louisiana didn't require them until 1914.

You can obtain vital registration certificates from the Department of Health or Vital Statistics for each state. Costs vary from state to state and may change frequently; for updated price and address information for any state, simply call your local Department of Health or see a pamphlet called "Where to Write for Vital Records: Births, Deaths, Marriages, and Divorces," published by the U.S. Department of Health & Human Services. Also, a CD-ROM called *Vital Records Archives* lists current addresses, phone numbers, and fees for the U.S. and its territories and the United Kingdom. This CD can automatically generate letters requesting records.

When you order a vital certificate, provide the individual's name, birth and death dates and places, and parents' names, if possible. Also, include your relationship and purpose ("family research" is fine). Some states are presently automating their vital records, but such projects may require years to complete, especially when large numbers are involved or interpreting early hand-written records is necessary. In the meantime, obtaining information which has yet to be computerized may take a long time. For instance, if you request vital statistics from New York, you may wait as long as a year for a response.

Table 6-1. Dates States Began Requiring Vital Registration

State	Birth/Death Records	Marriage/Divorce Records
Alabama	Jan 1908	8-1836 M; 1-1950 D
Alaska	1913	1913 M; 1950 D
Arizona	Jul 1909[1]	See Note 5
Arkansas	Feb 1914	1917 M; 1923 M
California	Jul 1905	Jul 1905 M; D (See Note 5)
Colorado	1910	none 1940-67
Connecticut	Jul 1897	Jul 1897 index M; 1947 D
Delaware	1861-3; 1881+	1847 M; 1935 D
Florida	Jan 1917[1]	6 Jun 1927
Georgia	Jan 1919	9 Jun 1962
Hawaii	1853	1853 M; Jul 1951 D
Idaho	1911	Jan 1947
Illinois	Jan 1916	Jan 1962
Indiana	Oct 1907 B; 1900 D	index 1958 M; D (See Note 5)
Iowa	Jul 1880	Jul 1880 M; 1906 D
Kansas	Jul 1911	May 1913 M; Jul 1951 D
Kentucky	Jan 1911	Jun 1958

State	Birth/Death Records	Marriage/Divorce Records
Louisiana	Jul 1914[2]	See Note 5
Maine	1892	Jan 1892
Maryland	Aug 1898[2]	Jun 1851 M; Jan 1961 D
Massachusetts	1841[2]	1841 M; index 1952 D
Michigan	1867[2]	Apr 1867 M; 1897 D
Minnesota	Jan 1809	index Jan 1958 M; Jan 1970 D
Mississippi	1912	1926-Jul 1938 & 1942 M; index 1926 D
Missouri	Jan 1910	index only, Jul 1948
Montana	late 1907	Jul 1943
Nebraska	late 1904	Jan 1909
Nevada	Jul 1911	index only, Jan 1968
New Hampshire	1640	1640 M; 1808 D
New Jersey	Jun 1878[3]	Jun 1878 M[3]; State Superior Court, D[3]
New Mexico	1920 ([1]1880)	See Note 5
New York	1880[2]	May 1915 M; Jan 1963 D
North Carolina	Oct 1913 B; Jan 1930 D	Jan 1962 M; Jan 1958 D
North Dakota	1920 ([2] from 1893)	See Note 5
Ohio	20 Dec 1908	See Note 5
Oklahoma	Oct 1908	See Note 5
Oregon	Jan 1903[2]	Jan 1906 M; 1925 D
Pennsylvania	Jan 1906[2]	Jan 1941 M; Jan 1946 D

State	Birth/Death Records	Marriage/Divorce Records
Rhode Island	1853	Jan 1853 M; State Clerk of Family Court D
South Carolina	Jan 1915[2]	Jul 1950 M; Jul 1962 D
South Dakota	Jul 1905	Jul 1905
Tennessee	Jan 1914[2]	Jul 1945
Texas	1903	Jan 1966 M; Jan 1968 D
Utah	1905[1]	1978
Vermont	see note 4	see note 4
Virginia	1853-96; 4 Jun 1912	Jan 1853 M; Jan 1918 D
Washington	Jul 1907	Jan 1968
West Virginia	Jan 1917	Jan 1921 M;1968 index D
Wisconsin	Oct 1907[1]	Oct 1907
Wyoming	Jul 1909	May 1941

1. Some earlier records or abstracts exist.
2. Records began earlier for at least one large city within the state.
3. Vital records from May 1848 to May 1878 are in state archives.
4. Has a nearly complete index to all vital records.
5. Records are at the county level only (no state records).

As you can see, vital registration is a relatively recent requirement in most states. Fortunately, counties (and towns in New England) often recorded births, marriages, and deaths long before the states began doing so. In some cases, county records date back to the creation of the jurisdiction, though usually with less complete coverage than that later required by state legislation. After you obtain available state certificates, you can check records in the appropriate county or town.

Most states have archived their early county, city, and town records, including vital records made before state registration. You'll probably need to visit the appropriate state archives to examine these records. In some states—Virginia, for example—county courthouses retain possession of the original records, and microfilmed duplicates are stored at the state archives. In other states—North Carolina, for example—counties may not have retained their own records; you must go to the state capital to see them.

The Family History Department of The Church of Jesus Christ of Latter-day Saints (or LDS church) has microfilmed many, though not all, of the early records in the state archives. Use the *Family History Library Catalog* (FHLC) to determine whether the records you seek are among them (see Chapter 4 for a discussion of the FHLC). If you are researching ancestry in your state of residence, ask a librarian about the possibility of obtaining state archives sources on loan.

Ancestry's Red Book lists vital and other records that are available at the county level. During your library research, check for published vital records; at the very least they provide a helpful index to the original records. The quality of published vital records depends on the conscientiousness and ability of their compilers. You may find some that contain notes added by a knowledgeable genealogist, which may be even more helpful than the original records. Nevertheless, published records often contain at least some errors or omissions; try to examine original records whenever possible.

Church Records

Historically, churches have often recorded marriages, christenings, and burials. Sometimes, they have also recorded births, deaths, and other events. Church records often predate and provide better information than contemporary government vital records. Churches that have historically kept good records include the Catholic church, New England Congregationalist, Quaker (a large colonial church), Moravian, German and Dutch Reformed, Lutheran, Episcopalian, and The Church of Jesus Christ of Latter-day Saints.

Because of the anti-English sentiment of the Revolutionary War era, many early official Anglican (later known as Protestant Episcopal) church records in the southern colonies were neglected, destroyed, or lost. The result is a lamentable gap in recorded information for this period. For example, no eighteenth-century North Carolina Anglican records are known to exist, and comparatively few early Virginia parish registers have survived.

Some church records are excellent, while some are disappointingly sparse. The difference depends at least as much on denominational record-keeping traditions as it does on the conscientiousness of individual ministers. Methodists, Baptists, and various evangelistic denominations, for example, often lack vital records, and those that do exist tend to be difficult to track down. A reference that may help you find vital church records is Kirkham's *Survey of American Church Records: Major and Minor Denominations Before*

1880-90. Another great resource that you can often find in larger libraries is Melton's *The Encyclopedia of American Religions.* If these sources indicate that a search will be tedious, or if your ancestor's denomination was notorious for poor record-keeping, you should search court, land, and census records first.

Ideally, you should have two pieces of information before using church records: Your ancestor's religious affiliation, and the location of records for that church. You may discover which church the individual belonged to through interviews with your relatives. Remember that church membership may not have remained constant through the generations. However, it was fairly common to have only one church in a town, so if you can't determine your ancestor's religion, begin by searching the records of the church that was predominant in the area and time period. To find the location of church records, write to the denomination (if the original church still exists). Even if the church no longer has its early records, its representatives may refer you to the present-day guardian of the records. Local historical societies, libraries, or archives may have them. For library research, use the "Church Records" and "Church Registers" subject headings to locate published and microfilmed church records.

Church records may be especially helpful if you're researching European ancestry. Most countries had national churches until a century or two ago, and the church records not only were well-kept, but also included a large segment of the population. In some countries and periods, almost the entire population is covered in the records of one national church. In other countries and periods, you may need to consider one or several non-conformist churches with large memberships. For instance, in addition to the three largest churches in Ireland (Roman Catholic, Established or Anglican, and Presbyterian), there were several other large dissenting groups (Baptists, Methodists, Huguenots, Methodists, and Quakers). However, political, legal, and historical factors often prompted Irish citizens to change or conceal their religious affiliation; if you can't find information for your ancestors among the records of the church to which you believe they belonged, check records for the state religion. As this example implies, in addition to determining the religious background of your ancestors, you should learn about the religious history of the country or area you are researching.

Cemetery Records

Cemetery records are another good source of vital statistics. They include tombstone inscriptions, sexton or custodian records, and mortuary records (including mortician and mausoleum records). Mortuary records are usually the most complete type of cemetery record, so use them whenever possible; they date back to the mid-nineteenth century. An annual publication called the

National Directory of Morticians lists the names and addresses of the mortuaries and funeral homes in the U.S. The directory is available at large libraries or through local mortuaries.

Many early cemetery records have been published in various secondary sources that you can find at the library or on the Internet. One excellent example is the database of cemetery inscriptions being compiled by the Ontario Cemetery Finding Association. More than 1.1 million inscriptions have been digitized, and you can download the compressed files from the association's homepage (http://www.island.net.com/ocfa/homepage.html).

You can obtain later records for immediate family members by requesting the records from the appropriate funeral home. For earlier periods, you should first consider sexton records for the town, city, and county, and sometimes for private or national cemeteries. These records are generally more complete and less prone to error than headstones. If your ancestor was buried in a church cemetery, as many people were in earlier times, look for the burial record among other church records.

Headstones and tombstones are worth checking, though many, disappointingly, show only initials, rather than names of the deceased, and many contain erroneous information. Many tombstone inscriptions (usually referred to as monumental inscriptions) have been transcribed and published. Those published by the Scottish Genealogical Society for pre-1855 cemeteries in Scotland are particularly impressive: Names are indexed and arranged by gravestone location; pertinent county and cemetery maps are included; and emblems, drawings, and other tombstone markings are described. Many books are less thorough, often consisting of only alphabetical listings.

In any case, nothing compares to actually viewing a headstone and the surrounding graves. Often, a careful study of family burials will reveal relationships. For example, the Joneses buried at one end of the cemetery are likely to be a different family from the Joneses at the other end. A Brown buried among a large group of Smiths probably had some family ties with them.

Tombstones may also be the only source for certain important facts, such as a maiden name, the original form of an Americanized surname, or data on children who died. In areas of great civil strife, such as parts of Ireland and the Southern states, tombstone records take on added value as the only remaining public record of the dead.

For these reasons, you should search local cemeteries in each known ancestral residence, if possible. Examine death certificates or obituary notices for each family member to learn which cemeteries were used by the family, then look up those locations in county histories or on older county or city maps. Chambers of commerce, city halls, elderly citizens, cemetery owners, and especially local funeral homes can help you find a particular cemetery.

Tombstone design styles can help you approximate the time of erection. This, in turn, helps you judge whether the death date recorded on a tombstone is primary or secondary evidence. Also, if you don't yet know the country of origin, you may find clues in family burial patterns, which varied among different ethnic groups. To learn more about burial patterns, see *The Source*, a book published by Ancestry Incorporated.

When you visit a cemetery, wear working clothes and old shoes or boots, avoid early morning or dusk if snakes may be a problem, and bring the following items:

- **Pen**

- **Paper**

- **Camera**

- **Artist's chalk:** Use chalk to complete letters in tombstone inscriptions to improve their legibility for photographs.

- **Pellon:** Place this non-woven fabric on very weathered, faint tombstone inscriptions to make rubbings; paper also works.

- **Crayons or charcoal:** Rub a crayon or piece of charcoal carefully over pellon (or paper) on the tombstone until the inscription appears.

- **Tweezers:** Use tweezers to remove lichen or other debris from the inscription.

- **Clippers or pruners:** Use clippers or pruners to remove branches and weeds.

Handle very old gravestones carefully. In the eastern U.S., the climate has worn away many of the most ancient inscriptions. Some have been restored, increasing the likelihood of errors in transcription. In Europe, on the other hand, you may find cemeteries that are several centuries old and still in fine condition.

Other Sources of Vital Statistics

Vital records, of course, are not infallible. Mistakes occur in every type of record. Generally, however, they occur less frequently in direct, primary sources—such as vital records—than elsewhere. For this reason, you should begin your original research with vital records.

Don't forget, though, that other record categories can sometimes yield secondary and even primary evidence regarding vital statistics. For example, the official Anglican church of pre-Revolutionary Virginia performed several civil functions, such as "processioning." This duty, which consisted of periodically walking over private property boundaries to retrace and confirm them (since aerial, photographic surveys were impossible), was assigned to landowners within the parish. A dated processioning record entry noting that John Smith became processioner when William Campbell died provides primary, direct evidence for William's death date. By referring to the earlier entry that appointed William to this assignment, you may narrow the time of his death to a period of a few weeks or even days. (Use the following notation to record a death date for a person known to be alive at one time and dead at another: "between 1 June 1800 and 27 July 1801." If the two dates refer to the date the will was written and the date it was recorded or proved, write, "w.d. [will dated] 1 June 1800, w.p. [will proved] 27 July 1801.")

A dated court-order book entry may read, "Thomas Nixon petitioned court for inheritance due his wife, Mary Stucky, from estate of her uncle Edmund Allen, dec'd." This provides evidence that Thomas and Mary were married before this time and that Stucky may be Mary's maiden name. It is more likely, however, that Stucky is her middle name or surname from an earlier marriage; more research is needed to determine which is the case. Earlier probate records or the will for Edmund Allen may yield additional facts about Mary's family.

If vital records aren't available for one or more of your ancestors, you should search every record category you can locate. But you will work with the law of averages by first checking out these more obvious sources.

Bibliography

Eichholz, Alice, ed. *Ancestry's Red Book: American State, County and Town Sources.* Rev. ed. Salt Lake City, UT: Ancestry, 1992.

Kirkham, E. Kay. *Survey of American Church Records: Major and Minor Denominations Before 1880-90.* 4th ed. Logan, UT: Everton Publishers, 1978.

Melton, J. Gordon. *The Encyclopedia of American Religions.* 3rd ed. Detroit, MI: Gale Research Co., 1989. Provides addresses and other information sources for more than 1,300 denominations.

National Directory of Morticians. Youngstown, OH: National Council of Morticians, annual.

Where to Write for Vital Records: Births, Deaths, Marriages, and Divorces. Hyattsville, MD: U.S. Dept. of Health and Human Services, 1991. To obtain a copy of this guide, write to Superintendent of Documents, U.S. Government Printing Office, Washington, DC 20402.

Chapter 7

Court, Land, and Census Records

You can find a wealth of genealogical data in court, land, and census records. Your research will progress significantly as you learn to take advantage of these resources.

Court Records

Courts create a variety of records involving events such as naturalization (see Chapter 8), divorce, trespass, debt, death, and so on. Whenever you learn of a situation likely to have resulted in litigation (such as a family feud or contested will), look for corresponding court records. England in particular has traditionally relied heavily upon its judicial system to resolve family quarrels. Colonial America not only followed this pattern, but produced even more voluminous—and often genealogically relevant—court proceedings, including many items now considered too trivial for legal action. Many colonial and early state court-order books have been microfilmed and are often worth searching page by page. During our research of colonial ancestors, we have noted that when a member of the propertied class died, several suits were typically filed within a short time, regardless of the existence of a will. Learning about the participants in those suits has often helped us determine family relationships.

Using Wills and Probates

Wills and probates are the court records you should generally check first; they often provide circumstantial or direct evidence of relationships. Testators often named married daughters or grandchildren in their wills, providing valuable evidence of family relationships. Unmarried or childless people often named nieces and nephews as heirs (a good reason to research the siblings of your ancestors).

However, not all children are necessarily named in a will, and sometimes no children are named. Children who died before their parent are obviously unlikely to be named, as are those who had already received their inheritance. If no children are named in an ancestor's will, look for deeds of gift made before the ancestor's death or quit-claim deeds made after. Quit-claim deeds usually named all then-living children. Also note instances of grandchildren being named as heirs in will or land records—they often were designated an inheritance in the place of deceased parents.

The eldest son may not be named in early English wills, as the law of primogeniture provided him automatic inheritance, unless otherwise specified in his father's will. This was also the case in the colonies of New York, New Jersey, Virginia, North and South Carolina, and Georgia through the Revolutionary War. Rhode Island abolished primogeniture in 1770. Maryland replaced it in 1715 with equal division: Each child received an equal share of the father's property if his will didn't specify otherwise. Pennsylvania, Delaware, and the New England colonies practiced a modified form of equal division, in which the eldest son received a double share.

The further back you extend your U.S. research, the more valuable wills become. Land and probate records were generally the only records considered important enough to keep during a period in which society's main concerns were surviving and conquering a wilderness. Because most early Americans were land holders, they often left wills. If they didn't, other probate records may still be helpful in research. Pay attention to the names of executors and administrators (refer to the Glossary of Legal Terms in the back of this book for definitions); in most cases they were close relatives, so knowing their names may help you substantiate pedigrees or expand your research.

Usually, you can find wills and probate records in the county where your ancestor died. Remember, widows and widowers often lived with or visited their children, so they may not have died in the place where they spent their earlier lives. Check *Ancestry's Red Book* for specifics such as which U.S. counties have probate records, the years these records cover, and the titles and addresses of the appropriate people to contact.

Wills and probate records are usually alphabetized and indexed by surname, so they are easy to locate, whether you visit a courthouse or examine a microfilmed index and request photocopies from the county clerk. A few indexes are not yet microfilmed; if you can't examine them personally, try requesting them through correspondence. Then cross your fingers—not all county clerks are cooperative. If you receive index entries, examine them to determine which might be worth photocopying. The Family History Department of The Church of Jesus Christ of Latter-day Saints (or LDS church) has microfilmed most indexes but few probate packets. These packets can be helpful enough to justify a personal courthouse visit.

Some counties have abstracted, indexed, and published their probate records. This can simplify and expand your research by enabling you to easily find other wills that mention your ancestors. Many maternal surnames can be uncovered in this manner. For example, suppose that your ancestors Edward and Sarah McMullen lived in Botetourt County, Virginia, in 1780. During your research, you learn that Botetourt County was an off-shoot of Augusta County, so you find Augusta County's pre-1800 court records, which have been abstracted, indexed, and published. In the index, you find a Sarah McMullen named as the daughter of James Robinson in his 1770 will. This could add a new line to your research. (Of course, you must rule out any other contemporary Sarah McMullens before concluding that this Sarah Robinson McMullen was your ancestor.)

Availability of Court Records

Numerous abstracts of early state court of appeals records have been published, and early court-order books and other records have been microfilmed or published as transcripts or abstracts. If the microfilming was done by the LDS Family History Department, you can find the films through the *Family History Library Catalog* (see Chapter 4). Records microfilmed by courts are located in state archives or county courthouse offices. Most modern court records are kept in their original jurisdictions, and each state has a separate and distinct court system. To locate such records for a specific state, you may need to consult an attorney who practices in that state.

Some excellent work has recently been completed by some states and counties to make court records accessible for research. One such state is Texas; its records are documented in Heskett's *Texas County Records: A Guide to the Holdings of the Local Records Division of the Texas State Library of County Records on Microfilm*. This work is arranged by county. Each county's boundaries are clearly identified and its date of creation, parent county, and county seat are named. Time periods for each type of record are noted, along with any omissions and available indexes. Property, probate, vital, court, tax, naturalization, and school records are covered, and background information for each is included. If you are searching for ancestral records in Texas, this extensive, quality research tool will make your research much easier.

Several states have computerized at least some county records. In Hamilton County, Ohio (which includes Cincinnati), workers have computerized 50,000 early documents—including wills (1791–1901) and naturalization papers (1837–1916)—and are in the process of computerizing hundreds of thousands of vital (birth and death) records dating back to 1865. For information on searching those databases, write to the following address:

University of Cincinnati
Archives and Rare Books Department
Eighth Floor—Blegen Library ML 113
Cincinnati, OH 45221

Other states that have computerized portions of county records include Illinois, Kansas, Iowa, Louisiana, Maine, and Pennsylvania. Unfortunately, some other states and counties delay or even restrict record use. As an extreme example, Michigan normally provides a copy of a birth certificate only if it is for your own birth or your child's birth. You should contact state libraries or check the Genealogical Projects Registry database, which is maintained by the National Genealogical Society with the LDS Family History Department (see Chapter 4 for details), for current information regarding computerization projects and requirements for accessing them.

Land Records

If you are researching U.S. ancestry in the colonial era, land records are an extremely useful source. Most colonists acquired property, and deeds often include genealogical information. In fact, it isn't unusual to find a chain of title in eighteenth-century and earlier deeds that extends a pedigree by several generations. Land records may also be valuable for European research. While there were fewer landowners in European countries, the names of tenant farmers and others working the land were often recorded in land records.

In the U.S., federal, state, and county jurisdictions have occasionally been involved in land sales. In colonial times, each colony handled land transactions differently.

Federal Land Records

After the Revolutionary War, several states that had claimed land west of the Mississippi River ceded it to the new national government as public domain. Other western land was later ceded to or purchased by the United States. The following states were formed from this area: Alabama, Alaska, Arkansas, Arizona, California, Colorado, Florida, Idaho, Illinois, Indiana, Iowa, Kansas, Louisiana, Michigan, Minnesota, Mississippi, Missouri, Montana, Nebraska, New Mexico, Nevada, North Dakota, Ohio, Oklahoma, Oregon, South Dakota, Utah, Washington, Wisconsin, and Wyoming. The land records in the National Archives consist principally of documents relating to the initial land sale or disposal in these states.

Finding Land Records

If your ancestor was the first settler on a piece of land in any of the above states, and if this ancestor bought the land from an entity other than a state government, speculator, or railroad, you can probably find the record of the original land purchase in the National Archives. Consult one of the following sources to learn about land records. (These sources also provide information for census, military, migration, and naturalization records.):

- *Guide to Genealogical Research in the National Archives.* 2nd ed. Washington, DC: National Archives Trust Fund Board, 1983.

- *Research Outline: United States.* Salt Lake City, UT: Family History Library, 1988. Considers many types of records for U.S. research, including detailed information on the history and use of land records. (Use the research outline for your state of interest for more detailed information.)

- Schaefer, Christina K. *The Center. A Guide to Genealogical Research in the National Capital Area.* Baltimore: Genealogical Publishing Co., 1996. A good reference for researching the excellent resources found in the U.S. capital, such as the National Archives, Library of Congress, the DAR Library, the National Genealogical Society, and many more.

- Szucs, Loretto Dennis, and Sandra Hargreaves Luebking. *The Archives: A Guide to the National Archives and Field Branches.* Salt Lake City, UT: Ancestry, 1988. An especially good guide for learning about and using the records found at the regional branches of the National Archives.

Federal land records date back to 1790, with most covering the span from 1800 to 1973. Little genealogical information is contained in land entry papers until the passage of the Homestead Act of 1862. Some other early federal land records have good information, though, including the donation entry files for Florida (1842–1850), Oregon, and Washington (1851–1903, with microfilmed indexes), and private land claims for parts of Alabama, Arizona, Arkansas, California, Colorado, Florida, Illinois, Indiana, Iowa, Louisiana, Michigan, Mississippi, Missouri, New Mexico, and Wisconsin. These private land claims consist of records of individuals who claimed grants from governments that owned land which eventually became part of the United States: the Northwest and Mississippi Territories, and the area that was included in the Louisiana Purchase as well as both the Florida and Mexican Cessions.

Land Records on CD-ROM
The General Land Office (GLO), part of the BLM, has automated more than 5 million land records made through 1908, including patents, plats, and field notes, that relate to the thirteen eastern public domain states. Entry began in 1991. These fragile, original documents are electronically scanned, then all data, including the scanned images, is entered into a searchable electronic database. The text portion of the database is being published on CD-ROM, state by state. CD-ROMs for Alabama, Arkansas, Louisiana, Florida, Michigan, Wisconsin, Minnesota, and Ohio are already available, while land records for the other eastern public domain states (Illinois, Indiana, Iowa, Mississippi, and Missouri) are being readied for publication. You may call the

GLO at 1-703-440-1600 to have your name put on a mailing list if you would like to be informed as each of these later states is completed.

The most recently published CD-ROMs in this series are more helpful and easier to use than the older ones because they use more and better help screens and sample files, and they are formatted more clearly. For example, homestead entry files in the new Ohio CD-ROM often include information taken from associated military, cash, or even United Brethren files—all of which provide information about the homesteader involved.

The cost of the *General Land Office Automated Patent System on CD-ROM* for each state is $15 ($14 for Alabama), including shipping. To use these CD-ROMs, you need a PC equipped with a color monitor and CD-ROM drive; they do not work on the Macintosh computer, nor in a Windows environment. (However, Family Tree Maker has compiled all the GLO records currently available into one Windows-compatible diskette costing $30; it does require their viewing software to run it. See chapter 12 for further details about Family Tree Maker CD-ROMs.) Operating instructions are printed on the back of the CD-ROM. To order, write to the following address:

Superintendent of Documents
P.O. Box 371954
Pittsburgh, PA 15250-7954

When you order, be sure to include the stock number of the CD for the state you want (see Table 7-1).

State Land Records

Land records for the thirteen original colonies are now kept at the state or local level. Many compilations and indexes have been published, and some are excellent. For example, in researching early Virginia families, we have found *Cavaliers and Pioneers: Abstracts of Virginia Land Patents and Grants* to be an invaluable resource. This is an ongoing, multivolume, indexed work of land records dating back to 1623 and earlier. When finally finished, it will reference over 100,000 genealogically pertinent entries. (Currently its volumes cover through the year 1749.) A similar series is now available for Maryland: *The Early Settlers of Maryland,* an index of names of immigrants, was compiled in 1968 by Gust Skordas from Maryland patent records, covering the years 1633-1680. But Peter Wilson Coldham, using the same series of Land Office books at the Maryland Hall of Records, just recently compiled five volumes in a *Settlers of Maryland* series that begins where Skordas left off. So coverage of the earliest Marylanders, as found in their land records, now extends through 1783.

Maine was part of Massachusetts until 1820; Vermont was part of New York until 1791; Kentucky and West Virginia were created from Virginia in 1792 and 1863, respectively; and Tennessee was created from North Carolina in 1792. You should look for the pre-statehood land records of these newer states in their parent state archives, rather than their own. Since Texas was a republic before it became a state, it held its own land records even before statehood—in its Spanish Archives, the Austin General Land Office contains indexed records dating back to 1745. The Daughters of the American Revolution Library in Washington, D.C. also houses a good collection of state and colonial land records and includes some that are indexed.

Table 7-1. States and Stock Numbers for the *General Land Office Automated Patent System* on CD-ROM

State	Stock Number
Alabama	024-011-00190-5
Arkansas	024-011-00181-6
Florida	024-011-00182-4
Louisiana	024-011-00183-2
Michigan	024-011-00185-9
Wisconsin	024-011-00186-7
Minnesota	024-011-00187-5
Ohio	024-011-00188-3

Note: If you visit BLM headquarters in the Washington, D.C. area or the BLM district offices in Jackson, Mississippi, and Milwaukee, Wisconsin, you can peruse the BLM database. You can also set up a remote account for online browsing of the database (for $2.00 per minute) by calling 1-703-440-1660. However, because most of the data is available on the state-specific CD-ROMs, you probably won't need to check the remainder of the database; if you do, you'll save money by completing as much prior research as possible on CD-ROM. The most cost-efficient way to retrieve any patent is by finding the document accession numbers on the CD-ROM, then providing these numbers on the menu's imaged order form. You can receive copies of the patents you need by mail or fax (1-703-440-1609) at a cost of $1.50 each.

The state of Illinois has electronically published a half-million of its original land records, including federal sales, from 1815 to 1880. This searchable database is linked to many genealogy World Wide Web sites (see Chapter 11 for information on the World Wide Web). You'll find some overlap between this information and the data on the GLO CD-ROM for Illinois (when it is published).

County Land Records

After the federally owned public domain land was sold, the state was responsible for subsequent sale and tax records. The deeds of these later sales are often indexed and held on the county level, where they are readily accessible in courthouses. You can search the *Family History Library Catalog* (FHLC) to find microfilmed indexes, or you can write to a county clerk to help you find the records you need.

Check *Ancestry's Red Book* to learn dates of extant county deeds and where to write for them. Generally, there are two sets of indexes: grantor (seller) and grantee (buyer). The first grantee deed may indicate, if not identify, the prior residence of a newcomer. Likewise, the last grantor deed may indicate the next residence of the seller, if the land was sold because the seller was leaving. Sometimes the entire history of the land's descent is provided, establishing genealogical descent as well.

Additional information in county land records includes names of the landowner's relatives (note that participating parties are often relatives), wife's given name (and occasionally maiden name), death date, occupation or other indications of social status, and perhaps circumstantial evidence for approximating dates of birth and marriage. If you are trying to establish descent through deeds, be sure to note the number of acres and the land description. Finding that same parcel of land in later generations (possibly divided up to accommodate several heirs) provides good circumstantial evidence of ancestry.

The earliest known county of residence is the logical place to begin a land record search. Evidence you find there may lead you to earlier county, federal, or state sources. If you can't find the original grantee deed for your ancestor's land, it was probably inherited. Look for evidence of this in wills or in a property division recorded under the surname. If you can't find anything in these sources, you can hypothesize that the land descended through the wife's family—you'll then search the same types of sources again under her maiden name. If your search is still unsuccessful, and if the wife was married previously, try searching under the married surname(s) as well.

County platte books, which contain old land surveys and related facts, can be very helpful. Often, you'll find power of attorney papers with county land records. Power of attorney papers furnish evidence of relationships and occasionally of family migration patterns. A power of attorney given by George Brown of Greenbrier, West Virginia, to Cyrus Brown to sell land in Kansas, provides circumstantial evidence of a relationship. It also names another county that you can include in your research—Greenbrier may be a prior residence of the Browns.

If all else fails, try tracing the associates of your ancestor to their place of origin. You may find your ancestor there, too, because extended families or even whole neighborhoods often migrated together. While this probably was most common for Germanic peoples, it was fairly common for British families as well. We have been happily surprised at the number of very early immigrants to Virginia and elsewhere that we have been able to connect, at least tentatively, to their English, Scottish, and Irish antecedents by using this approach.

Census Records

Because most census records are indexed and provide a plethora of genealogical information about everyone in a particular household, they can help you determine basic, crucial information about your ancestors, such as their birth dates and places of residence.

1790–1840

Though early American census records don't provide the names and birthplaces of those enumerated, they do disclose the names of heads of households, along with the number, genders, and approximate ages of all others in the household. The age-grouping data can often help you determine ages of family members as you trace them through successive censuses. Because these early censuses are now indexed, you don't need to know your ancestors' place of residence to begin your search; you can use the indexes to find ancestors even if you know only their names.

Several states, however, are missing portions of their federal censuses. For Virginia, Kentucky, Georgia, Tennessee, New Jersey, and Delaware, various other records—mostly state tax records—of a corresponding period have been indexed and substituted for the missing 1790 census returns. Tax records supplement census records by naming unmarried property owners or property owners living with families other than their own. Censuses, on the other hand, include even nonpropertied families. Some names not included on one type of record may be found on the other, so you may want to search them both, if possible.

Although it is not an actual census, Schreiner-Yantis and Love's *The 1787 Census of Virginia* is an example of the excellent information in some early state tax/census records. While it consists only of tax list returns, the book actually contains more information than the missing 1790 census. Because it includes present-day Kentucky and West Virginia counties, and because Virginia was by far the largest state during that period, *The 1787 Census of Virginia* is a monumental work—it covers one-fifth of the entire U.S. population at that time. Having used it extensively in our eighteenth-century research, we have come to appreciate both the meticulousness of the compilers and the computer technology that helped them complete the project.

1850–1870

Beginning with the 1850 census, the names, ages, and birthplaces of everyone enumerated are included, as well as the occupation of males older than fifteen, the value of real estate, and other helpful items. Thus, the federal censuses from 1850 and later enable us to reconstitute family groups at least provisionally, and often completely. Each state's 1850 census is now indexed, increasing its research value. The 1860 census includes the same type of information as the 1850 census and adds the value of personal property. The 1870 census is the first census that contains information about immigrant progenitors. It uses the word *foreign* to indicate that the parents of enumerated individuals were born abroad. Several states have published abstracts of census records from 1850 through 1870. The Tennessee 1850 and 1860 censuses, the West Virginia 1880 census, and some other states' censuses have been abstracted and published as books.

The following organizations offer indexing services and products:

Precision Indexing
P.O. Box 254
Bountiful, UT 84011

This firm claims about one-third more names than comparable indexes and offers hardbound, fiche, and floppy disk copies of the following federal census indexes: 1848–50 Ontario, Canada; 1860 California, Connecticut, Delaware, Washington, D.C., Florida, Kentucky, Oregon, Rhode Island, and South Carolina (every-name); 1870 Delaware, Washington, D.C., Florida (every-name), Georgia, North Carolina, Pennsylvania (divided into East and West), Oregon, Rhode Island, South Carolina, Virginia, West Virginia, Kentucky, Chicago, St. Louis, and Long Island; 1880 Ohio; 1910 Nevada and Wyoming; 1890 Civil War Pensioner's census indexes for Kentucky, Louisiana, Maine, Maryland, Massachusetts, Michigan, Minnesota, Mississippi, New York, and Texas.

Genealogical Services
P.O. Box 890
West Jordan, UT 84084
(801) 280-1554
E-mail: info@genservices.com

Genealogical Services publishes all of the U.S. federal, territorial, and state census indexes, as well as tax records and other genealogical records. Some of these records are available on CD-ROM.

1880

The 1880 census provides direct evidence of the relationship of each member of the household to the head of the household. (Keep in mind, however, that the wife of a male head of household is not necessarily the mother of all, or any, of his children.) This census also lists the state or country of birth of enumerated individuals and their parents. If this information was reported accurately, it will help you trace further generations; however, it may not be trustworthy. For example, in a Tennessee family we researched, a man reported his mother's state of birth as Alabama at the same time that she, living as a widow within his household, reported it as Tennessee. On an earlier census, she reported her state of birth as Virginia!

The 1880 census also has a partial Soundex index, meaning that all names that sound alike are placed together. The Soundex covers all families with children aged 10 or younger. Microfilmed copies are available through the LDS Family History Library, the National Archives, and their respective branches. The LDS Family History Department is indexing the 1880 U.S. census; by the end of 1996, the extractions for that project were nearly complete. The history department at the University of Minnesota compiled a one-percent sampling of the 1880 census, and online genealogist Michael Cooley published the genealogically relevant information from that sampling to separate electronic files for each household involved (more than 107,000 households were included in the sampling). To obtain access to any of these files, you may send a request by electronic mail (e-mail) to the following address: 1880@genealogy.emcee.com.

Mortality Schedules 1850-1880

Special schedules accompanied various censuses. Some that may be helpful include Agricultural and Manufacturing/Industrial schedules. The most popular and accessible schedules are the mortality schedules that accompanied the 1850-1880 censuses. They provide detailed data for individuals who died within the previous year. Mortality schedules constitute one of the microfiched Accelerated Indexing Systems (AIS) Indexes available at LDS family history centers (see Chapter 4 for more information on AIS). The Banner Blue division of Brøderbund has also compiled some mortality schedules on CD-ROM.

1890 and Later

Unfortunately, the 1890 census was destroyed, with the exception of some returns for counties (about one percent of the total census) and a schedule of Civil War Union veterans or their widows living in states alphabetically from Kentucky (partial) to Wyoming. The veteran schedules are available from Precision Indexing.

Genealogical societies in Arkansas and California are coordinating extensive volunteer efforts to gather and publish records to substitute for their missing 1890 federal censuses. The recent discovery of 1890 voting records for Chicago provides a similar resource to help fill the gap. Smaller-scale projects have been completed or are in progress at several county levels; check with your local genealogical society for details about projects in your area of interest.

The 1900–1920 censuses are available on microfilm. The 1900 census is the only one that provides the month and year of birth for all individuals enumerated. It is also completely indexed, as is the 1920 census. The 1900 and 1910 censuses show number of years married, number of previous marriages, total number of children borne by the wife, how many children are then living, Civil War veteran status, and, where applicable, year of immigration and some naturalization facts for adult males.

The 1910 census has been indexed for only 21 states: Alabama, Arkansas, California, Florida, Georgia, Illinois, Kansas, Kentucky, Louisiana, Michigan, Missouri, Mississippi, North Carolina, Ohio, Oklahoma, Pennsylvania, South Carolina, Tennessee, Texas, Virginia, and West Virginia. Missing indexes will probably be published eventually by private publishers, as they recently have been for some states with relatively small populations, including Hawaii, Nevada, and Wyoming.

The 1920 census does not provide all the data that the 1900 census does. However, it supplies immigration and naturalization data not only for adult males, but for all others enumerated as well. People born in Eastern Europe were often very meticulous in their specifications of birthplace for this census—because World War I had caused so many boundary changes, enumerators were instructed to request the name of the province or city of birth for individuals or parents born in Germany, Austria-Hungary, Russia, or Turkey.

Privacy laws prohibit releasing more recent census data. However, you may request some information from census records made after 1920 by completing a form called the Application for Search of Census Records. To obtain the form, write to the following address:

U.S. Department of Commerce
Bureau of the Census
P.O. Box 1545
Jeffersonville, IN 47131

State and Colonial Censuses

States, colonies, counties, and cities sometimes conducted their own censuses. New York has thirty-two colonial and state censuses taken between 1663 and 1925, for example. Early state censuses have been indexed and published, while microfilmed copies available through the Family History Library and card indexes located in the New York State Archives exist for some of the later ones. The New York state censuses for 1855, 1865, and 1875 record facts not found elsewhere, such as those who had married or died during the previous year. Such additional state censuses may exist for your state of interest; check the FHLC, the chapter on census records found in *The Source,* or consult Lainhart's *State Census Records,* a recently published book that provides a comprehensive inventory of state censuses.

Accessibility of Census Records

Part of the value of the federal censuses and their indexes lies in their easy accessibility. Many city and county libraries have purchased the censuses for their own states, and often those for adjoining states as well. Your local librarian can help you locate nearby libraries that have copies of the censuses you need. You can also rent census records from LDS family history centers and rent or buy them through commercial sources.

The American Genealogical Lending Library (AGLL) has the largest collection of national, state, county, and local records on microfilm and microfiche available to the public. They can be ordered by libraries and individuals. For membership information and a recent catalog, write to the following address:

AGLL
P.O. Box 244
Bountiful, UT 84011

You may also order copies of census records from libraries that participate in the National Archives microfilmed census program. Contact your local librarian for details. In some cases, purchasing records is more economical than renting them—for instance, you may want to review a particular set of records whenever you discover related surnames.

Census Searching Tips

To locate a census entry quickly, use a census index. As a check against possible errors, use all available indexes—you can find published or microfilmed indexes in many large libraries. Record all data verbatim for every name in the ancestral household and for neighbors who may be related. If you are unsuccessful in your initial search for a family in a census, you may need to conduct a second, more thorough search. Recheck each entry to make sure it is *not* the desired one. By using this method on a Canadian census, we were able to find our Cosgriff family—because the family appeared under the name Coskery, we had overlooked it initially.

Check each census in which a family might appear to find additional facts and estimate probable ages, especially adult ages, which have often been inaccurately reported. Search sheets, available at genealogical supply centers, enable more rapid and accurate recording because they follow the columnar format of each census.

Excessive fading or damage sometimes makes it difficult, if not impossible, to read certain census entries. Microfilm image enhancement technology, however, helps eliminate the effects of aging to restore readability. Specialized microfilm printers based on that technology are already in use (one is available to patrons in the university library where this author works, for example). Genealogical CD publishers also use this technology to eliminate the scratches and smudges found on original microfilmed records which they then publish as CD-ROMs. One such project will be detailed in chapter 12.

Records for Other Countries

Microfilmed census records exist for many countries. You can locate them through the FHLC. Microfilmed census records for Spanish-speaking countries begin earlier and contain more complete information than the censuses of English-speaking countries.

Canadian Records

The National Archives of Canada offers a CD-ROM that includes the index to the 1871 Ontario census, which was created by the Ontario Genealogical Society (OGS). The information on the CD-ROM is also available in books published by the OGS and as computer files through the following sources: The National Capital Freenet in Ottawa (telnet freenet.carleton.ca); some genealogical bulletin boards and File Transfer Protocol (FTP) sites; and a

World Wide Web page (http://www.archives.ca/db/1871/Introduction.html). Since the files require considerable disk storage space when uncompressed, the CD-ROM version may be more convenient; however, the CD-ROM database requires you to search each county separately for names, while the Internet site allows you to search the entire database by key word.

The National Archives of Canada will publish upon demand a CD-ROM that contains the heads of households for the 1871 census of Ontario. Because the files have been recorded in ASCII text, you can read them with any word processor or with one of the viewers included with the CD-ROM. The files are arranged geographically by census district and contain the name, gender, age, country of origin, religion, ethnic origin, and occupation of the heads of the households, and the corresponding census page number. This same information is also available for online searching and downloading, or as hard copy.

> The National Archives of Canada
> Reference Services
> 395 Wellington Street
> Ottawa, Ontario, Canada K1A 0N3

English, Welsh, and Scottish Records

The 1841 census of England, Wales, and Scotland is the first census to report each person's name, age, occupation, and country of birth. From 1851 to the present, census records include individuals' relationship to the head of the household, marital status, and English county or foreign country of birth. The 1841–1891 censuses are microfilmed or microfiched and, along with some indexes (most of them only partial), are available through the FHLC and the Internet. The LDS Family History Department recently helped coordinate a large-scale extraction project of the 1881 British census. The information available on microfiche consists of several indexes, including surname, birthplace, census place, and "as enumerated." These indexes will soon be available on CD-ROM as well. (See Chapter 12 for more details.)

In 1993, several computerized English, Welsh, and Scottish partial census transcripts, along with a list of all surnames in those transcripts, were entered into the genealogy section of a public electronic directory that you can access through the Internet by using the address essex.ac.uk. The data has also been transferred to many other genealogy bulletin boards worldwide. As a harbinger of future possibilities, we expect an increasing amount of such raw genealogical data to become available by modem for research and retrieval.

Bibliography

Cavaliers and Pioneers: Abstracts of Virginia Land Patents and Grants, 1623–1800. Vols. 1-3 edited by Nell Marion Nugent. Richmond, VA: Press of the Dietz Print Co., 1934. Vols. 4 and 5 edited by Denis Hudgen. Richmond, VA: Virginia Genealogical Society, 1994.

Coldham, Peter Wilson. *Settlers of Maryland*. 5 vols. Baltimore: Genealogical Publishing Co., 1995.

Guide to Genealogical Research in the National Archives. 2nd ed. Washington, DC: National Archives Trust Fund Board, 1983.

Heskett, Michael. *Texas County Records: A Guide to the Holdings of the Local Records Division of the Texas State Library of County Records on Microfilm*. 2nd ed. Austin, TX: Texas State Library, Local Records Division, 1990.

Lainhart, Ann S. *State Census Records*. Baltimore, MD: Genealogical Publishing Co., 1992.

Research Outline: United States. Salt Lake City, UT: Family History Library, 1988.

Schaefer, Christina K. *The Center. A Guide to Genealogical Research in the National Capital Area*. Baltimore: Genealogical Publishing Co., 1996.

Schreiner-Yantis, Netti, and Florene Love. *The 1787 Census of Virginia*. Springfield, VA: Genealogical Books in Print, 1987.

Skordas, Gust. *The Early Settlers of Maryland. An Index of Names of Immigrants Compiled from Records of Land Patents, 1633-1680, in the Hall of Records, Annapolis, Maryland*. Reprint. Baltimore: Genealogical Publishing Co., 1995.

Szucs, Loretto Dennis, and Sandra Hargreaves Luebking. *The Archives: A Guide to the National Archives and Field Branches*. Salt Lake City, UT: Ancestry, 1988.

Chapter 8

Military, Naturalization, and Immigration Records

Military Records

Military records are an important source of genealogical information. Among the millions of records documenting those who have served in the American armed forces, service and pension records are most useful to genealogists. Libraries with strong genealogical collections generally house microfilmed copies of military records predating the Revolutionary War.

National Archives

Most military records created from the Revolutionary War to World War I have been preserved and made available by the National Archives. Many of the most popular military records have been microfilmed and indexed. National Archives researchers will search indexed military records for a minimum fee (to cover the cost of photocopies). Requests for military service and pension records from before World War I should be submitted on NATF Form 80. You may obtain this form by writing to the following address:

> The National Archives and Records Administration
> General Reference Branch
> Washington, D.C. 20408

In some cases, you may not be able to complete the entire form; however, you should provide as much information as possible to help researchers locate the file. Be sure to request all military service records and documents; otherwise, you may receive copies of only selected documents.

You can find many of the microfilmed indexes, along with other military documents, at the regional branches of the National Archives and in other major genealogical collections, including the Family History Library operated by The Church of Jesus Christ of Latter-day Saints (or LDS church; see Chapter 4 for more information about the Family History Library). The National Archives' *Military Service Records: A Select Catalog of National Archives Microfilm Publications* itemizes microfilms such as the *Index of Revolutionary War Pension Applications in the National Archives*. Neagles' *U.S. Military Records: A Guide to Federal and State Sources, Colonial*

America to the Present is a comprehensive reference that lists the types of records you'll find in the National Archives and in state and private libraries and archives.

Microfilmed copies of pension records from the War of 1812 (1812–1815) and the Mexican War (1846–1848) are available at the National Archives and some of its regional branches (see Appendix C), and at the LDS Family History Library. The National Archives also has pensioners' indexes for the Old Wars (1815) and the Indian Wars (1892–1926).

Records from World War I are described in *Guide to Genealogical Research in the National Archives*, published by the National Archives Trust Fund Board. Other valuable sources for World War I are draft registration cards. All males from twenty-one to thirty-one years of age were required to register for the draft in 1917. By the final draft call in 1918, the age range had expanded to include all men from eighteen to forty-five years of age. Most of the resulting 24 million World War I Selective Service records—which cover approximately twenty-three percent of the U.S. population in 1918—are available on microfilm at LDS family history centers. The cards are arranged alphabetically by state (including Alaska, Hawaii, Puerto Rico, and the District of Columbia), then by local draft board, which generally corresponds to the county or city. However, in Connecticut, Massachusetts, and Rhode Island, registrants appear in one alphabetical list for the entire state. Searching for a name in these states or in rural or low-density population areas usually is simple, but in large cities and counties with several draft boards—189 in New York City, for example—finding the name you're looking for may be more difficult. You may need to consult a 1917 city directory to find the individual's street address so you can determine the appropriate draft board.

Civil War Records

The Civil War, which involved more soldiers than any other war in which the U.S. has participated, generated numerous records for Union military personnel and even some civilians. A massive national indexing project sponsored by the National Archives, National Park Service, Genealogical Society of Utah, and Federation of Genealogical Societies will simplify Civil War research: Volunteers throughout the country are entering the names of millions of Civil War soldiers into a database that will be available in many locations. For more information on this indexing project, write to the following address:

Federation of Genealogical Societies Business Office
P.O. Box 830220
Richardson, TX 75083-0220

The Civil War *Roll of Honor* is another great resource. This twenty-seven-volume work lists burials to over a quarter-million Union soldiers in over three hundred national cemeteries. It was originally published by the U.S. government shortly after the Civil War ended. A consolidated ten-volume re-issue of this monumental work was published in 1994, followed in 1995 by a 1200-page index to it. (See bibliography.)

Recent Records

To obtain copies of military records for individuals who served in the armed forces during and after World War I, you should complete Standard Form 180 and submit it to the following address:

National Personnel Records Center
9700 Page Boulevard
St. Louis, MO 63132-5100

Other Resources

Individual states can be rich sources for military information. Some state archives and historical agencies maintain indexes of individuals from the state who have served in wars. State agencies frequently retain copies of published works that focus on citizens' participation in military events. You may also find general military works such as White's *Genealogical Abstracts of Revolutionary War Pension Files* in state agencies.

The Daughters of the American Revolution (DAR) have compiled a great deal of information on individuals who performed any service, including nonmilitary service, during the American Revolution. Proportionate to the population, more people served in the Revolutionary War than in any other U.S.-involved conflict. Many women and exceptionally old and young men were involved. Because the U.S. government did not make pensions or land grants available to the surviving veterans or their heirs until many years after the war, many veterans died before becoming eligible for government benefits. The service of these nonpensioned veterans, as well as war casualties and others who performed nonmilitary service, may be documented only in the widely available *Lineage Books* and *Patriot Index* published by the DAR.

Another good recent resource is Bockstruck's *Revolutionary War Bounty Land Grants Awarded by State Governments*. It indexes some 35,000 names of Revolutionary War soldiers and citizens (or heirs who claimed under their names) who served in the states of Connecticut, Georgia, Maryland, Massachusetts, New York, North Carolina, Pennsylvania, South Carolina, and Virginia.

International Records

You may be able to find records for ancestors who served in the militaries of other countries. Because military service is mandatory (or has been at some point) in some regions of the world, you may find records for a large percentage of the population. Internationally, military records are frequently more detailed than those in the U.S.

Great Britain, Germany, France, and the Russian and Austrian Empires used military censuses to identify people who were eligible for military service. Muster rolls, which were generally implemented in the mid-seventeenth century, provide helpful genealogical data and often such descriptive information as the soldier's complexion, height, and eye color. Use the *Family History Library Catalog* (FHLC) and the subject heading "Military Records" to locate muster rolls for particular countries. (See Chapter 4 for more information on the FHLC.)

Naturalization Records

The process of becoming a citizen is called naturalization. Naturalization documents are often excellent sources of genealogical information. The National Archives in Washington, D.C. houses citizenship documents for individuals who were naturalized in the District of Columbia. Naturalization records for people who became citizens in federal courts are stored in the regional branches of the National Archives. Each region holds documents for courts in the states it serves. Some regions have extensive naturalization indexes that include local courts. These indexes may be helpful, especially if you don't know the date or court of naturalization. The National Archives–Great Lakes Region, for example, has an index of over a million and a half names of individuals naturalized in federal and local courts in Illinois, Indiana, Iowa, and Wisconsin, compiled by the Work Projects Administration (WPA). Research guides such as the National Archives' *Guide to Genealogical Research in the National Archives* and Szucs and Luebking's *The Archives: A Guide to the National Archives Field Branches* provide information on naturalization records by state.   The LDS Family History Library has microfilmed copies of many of the major naturalization indexes, as well as smaller indexes that list naturalizations in state, county, and local courts.

Several types of naturalization records have been described, indexed, and published in genealogical and historical periodicals. The PERiodical Source Index (PERSI) contains a comprehensive place, subject, and surname index to current and past articles appearing in more than two thousand periodicals. PERSI is a practical tool for locating naturalization topics and indexes that have appeared in print. (See Chapter 4 for more information on PERSI.)

Availability of Records

The Bureau of Immigration, established in 1906, standardized naturalization procedures and forms—most naturalizations after 1906 took place in federal courts. However, if you're looking for records of naturalizations granted before September 27, 1906, you may have difficulty finding them because people could receive citizenship in any court of record.

Voting lists often pinpoint the court and date of an individual's naturalization. If you can't locate naturalization documentation, you should check with city and county offices to determine if voting lists are available—unfortunately, not all local governments have kept them.

1776 and Earlier

A few naturalization records prior to 1777—mostly oaths of allegiance—have been published. Examples include Stevenson's "Persons Naturalized in New Jersey, 1702-1766," in *New York Genealogical & Biographical Record* and Wyland's *Colonial Maryland Naturalizations*. Such publications cover a very small percentage of the population because the British government did not require proof of citizenship from residents of the colonies. In the absence of naturalization documentation, you can sometimes find mention of immigrants' places of origin in county court records, family Bibles, letters, histories or traditions, voting rolls, land or property records, newspapers, and military documents.

Revolutionary War Period to 1906

Few naturalization records exist before 1802, when the U.S. government began requiring immigrants to register with a local court upon arrival in the U.S. (This requirement was repealed in 1828.) Individuals' countries of origin and dates of registration may be the only information included in early records. For example, a court-order book may state, "On this 6th day of June, 1804, John Anderson renounces forever all allegiance and fidelity to any foreign prince, potentate, state or sovereignty whatever, and particularly to the King of Sweden of whom he was a subject."

Although naturalization statutes changed several times prior to 1906 and documents vary significantly from court to court and year to year, generally the law required immigrants to be residents of the United States for at least five years before they could become citizens. People could be naturalized in the nearest court, even if it was not located in their county of residence. Some courts maintain good indexes to naturalizations; others may have indexes for only a few years or none at all.

Several federal censuses (1820, 1830, 1870, 1900, 1910, and 1920) and some state censuses provide citizenship status data. The 1920 census is especially good for obtaining both immigration and naturalization dates (see Chapter 7). Also, the National Archives–New England Region has an index published by the WPA, *Index to New England Naturalization Petitions 1791-1906*, that cites documents for individuals who became citizens in federal, state, county, and local courts in Connecticut, Maine, Massachusetts, Rhode Island, Vermont, and New Hampshire.

In most cases, you can find declarations of intention and final citizenship papers at the county courthouse in the county that issued them. If microfilmed indexes and court records aren't available, you may need to visit the county courthouse. Try to find a cooperative clerk to help you locate naturalization documents.

1906 and Later

As a result of the Bureau of Immigration's standardization of citizenship procedures and forms in September 1906, naturalization records after this period are easier to locate and contain more valuable genealogical information than earlier records. These records usually consist of three sets of documents: declarations of intention, petitions, and certificates of naturalization and oaths of allegiance.

- **Declarations of intention (first papers):** Declarations of intention issued after 1906 generally include the immigrant's full name, age, occupation, personal description, place and date of birth, citizenship, present address, and prior address (before emigration), along with the name of the vessel and port of embarkation and arrival, application date, name of the naturalizing court, and, finally, the immigrant's signature.

- **Petitions:** Petitions issued after 1906 generally include the petitioner's full name, address, occupation, date and place of birth, citizenship, personal description, emigration date, port of embarkation and arrival, and marital status. If the petitioner had dependents (that is, spouse and/or children), their names, ages, and birthplaces are also included, as well as their emigration date, the ship of entry's name, port of embarkation and arrival, names and addresses of witnesses, and duration of residence in the state. After 1930, photographs of petitioners are also included.

- **Certificates of naturalization and oaths of allegiance:** Certificates of naturalization and oaths of allegiance issued after 1906 usually provide the new citizen's full name, address, nationality or place of birth, birth date or age, and country of emigration. To obtain information and copies of documents for individuals who were naturalized after September 27, 1906, inquiries should be sent to:

Immigration and Naturalization Service
425 Eye Street NW
Washington, D.C. 20536

Naturalization Procedures

Most immigrants who obtained citizenship began naturalization procedures as soon as they met the five-year residency requirement. However, others did not file their first papers until they had been in the U.S. for many years. Some immigrants took out papers in their first place of residence but finalized citizenship in a different county or state. Until 1922, wives and minor children derived citizenship from their husbands or fathers. Certain groups were not allowed citizenship—the Chinese were excluded for the longest period. Even the restrictive Chinese Exclusion laws, however, required extensive records; thousands are housed at the National Archives–Pacific Sierra Region. For information on these records (now being extracted and added into a Chinese Immigration Database organized so that a name can be retrieved by any one of its three Chinese characters—these characters being converted into a numeric code somewhat analogous to a Soundex system), contact one of the regional offices involved. (Appendix C lists addresses for regional branches of the National Archives.)

Immigration Records

All Americans, even Native Americans, emigrated from elsewhere at some point. The earlier your ancestors came to the Americas, the more difficult it may be to trace their origins. However, in recent years, myriad scattered passenger and immigration lists have been compiled and indexed—these lists can help you find information on early immigrants. One of the largest published indexes is Filby's *Passenger and Immigration Lists Index*, which is particularly strong for the years prior to 1825 and adds supplements annually.

More immigration data is becoming available for the late nineteenth century. Under the direction of Dr. Ira Glazier, Director of the Balch Center of Immigration Research at Temple University, data from original passenger lists is being indexed. Ultimately, the index will list the names of some 35 million immigrants who came to America by ship from 1820 to 1924.

The first Balch project published Glazier's *Famine Immigrants: Lists of Irish Immigrants Arriving at the Port of New York, 1846–1851*, a seven-volume set of previously unindexed lists of Irish immigrants. Data for Germans—the largest nineteenth-century U.S. immigrant group—who arrived after 1850 is being published in Glazier and Filby's *Germans to America* series. Now containing fifty volumes, it is close to completing its goal of recording the 4 million German immigrants who arrived through 1917. Presently, the information is current up to 1884. The series eventually will include data through 1917 for more than 4 million U.S. immigrants from Germany. Glazier and Filby's *Italians to America* Balch series is a five-volume index of names of Italian emigrants who came to the U.S. from 1880 through 1891. Volumes six and seven have just recently become available as well. Another series, *Migrations from the Russian Empire,* began publication in 1995. The first two volumes in this series contain data on over 100,000 persons of Russian nationality arriving in New York ports between 1875 and 1886.

The LDS Family History Department recently began a project to computerize passenger arrival records of Ellis Island, or the Port of New York. They are extracting much of the important genealogical information about all aliens, U.S. citizens returning home from European travel, crew members, and stowaways in these 1897-1924 records. Look for them to be completed in about 1998.

Before attempting to trace immigrants' origins, you should read a useful pamphlet titled *Tracing Immigrant Origins,* available at the LDS Family History Library and some LDS family history centers. Szucs and Luebking's *The Source: A Guidebook of American Genealogy* contains a strong chapter on immigration sources and methodology. Avoid researching immigrant families' countries of origin too soon. First, search U.S. records to try to determine either the families' specific residences in the countries from which they emigrated, or the names of their relatives and associates in those countries.

We have located many early-seventeenth-century immigrants from Great Britain by searching early court and land records for names of the immigrants' associates—both before and after immigration—and overseas place names.

Through the microfilming program of the LDS Family History Department, more records from Europe and other places are becoming available at LDS family history centers in the U.S., increasing the possibility of conducting successful overseas research without leaving this country.

We expect great breakthroughs in immigration-emigration research before the end of the decade. Already, the Internet provides a continually improving system whereby researchers from practically anywhere in the world can pool their efforts and share their knowledge. Such enhanced international cooperation will help resolve many immigrant-emigrant questions that currently are enigmatic.

Bibliography

Bockstruck, Lloyd D. *Revolutionary War Bounty Land Grants Awarded by State Governments.* Baltimore: Genealogical Publishing Co., 1996.

Filby, P. William, with Mary K. Meyer and Dorothy M. Lower. *Passenger and Immigration Lists Index: A Guide to Published Arrival Records of . . . Passengers who Came to the United States and Canada in the Seventeenth, Eighteenth, and Nineteenth Centuries.* 17 vols, annual supplements. Detroit, MI: Gale Research Co., 1981-95. Consult this book first for pre-1825 immigrant records. It contains several million names and is very well done, easy to use, and widely available.

Glazier, Ira A., and P. William Filby, eds. *Germans to America: Lists of Passengers Arriving at U.S. Ports.* Wilmington, DE: Scholarly Resources, 1988–95.

—. *Italians to America: Lists of Passengers Arriving at U.S. Ports, 1880–1899.* Wilmington, DE: Scholarly Resources, 1992–95.

Glazier, Ira A., ed. *The Famine Immigrants: Lists of Irish Immigrants Arriving at the Port of New York, 1846–1851.* Baltimore, MD: Genealogical Publishing Co., 1983–86.

Guide to Genealogical Research in the National Archives. 1982. Rev. ed. Washington, DC: National Archives and Records Administration, 1985.

Military Service Records: A Select Catalog of National Archives Microfilm Publications. Washington, DC: National Archives Trust Fund Board, National Archives and Service Administration, 1985.

Neagles, James C. *U.S. Military Records: A Guide to Federal and State Sources, Colonial America to the Present.* Salt Lake City, UT: Ancestry, 1994.

Reamy, Martha, and William Reamy, comps. *Index to the Roll of Honor.* Baltimore: Genealogical Publishing Co., 1996.

Stevenson, J.R. "Persons Naturalized in New Jersey, 1702-1766." *New York Genealogical & Biographical Record,* vol. 28, 1897.

Szucs, Loretto Dennis, and Sandra Hargreaves Luebking, eds. *The Source: A Guidebook of American Genealogy.* Rev. ed. Salt Lake City, UT: Ancestry, 1996.

Szucs, Loretto Dennis, and Sandra Hargreaves Luebking. *The Archives: A Guide to the National Archives Field Branches.* Salt Lake City, UT: Ancestry, 1988.

United States Quartermaster's Department. *Roll of Honor.* Baltimore: Genealogical Publishing Co., 1994-. A serial publication containing Civil War Union burials. Originally published by the Government Printing Office, Washington, DC, 1865-1871.

White, Virgil D. *Genealogical Abstracts of Revolutionary War Pension Files.* 4 vols. Waynesboro, TN: National Historical Publishing Co., 1990-92.

Wyland, Jeffrey A., and Florence L. Wyant. *Colonial Maryland Naturalizations.* Baltimore, MD: Genealogical Publishing Co., 1975.

Chapter 9

Basic Computer Hardware

Some genealogists become so infatuated with computer technology that they lose sight of the fact that it is just a tool to help them get their work done. On the other hand, for computer technology to enhance your genealogical research, you need a good grasp of basic technological information. We hope this chapter will provide you with much necessary background, but a specialized book on personal computers and computer genealogy may also be helpful. Many books at your local library or bookstore provide basic information about the personal computer (PC and/or Macintosh). Such references can help get you through the initial rough spots and teach you the jargon ("technobabble") that you will inevitably encounter and eventually start using.

Choosing a Computer

Computers have gone beyond the work place; they can now be purchased in both traditional and discount department stores—even furniture stores carry them. To make a wise purchase, you must have some knowledge of the equipment involved.

If this is your first exposure to the home computer, you probably don't need the fastest machine, or the one with the most memory or the largest disk drive. On the other hand, a machine that is several years old may require you to invest considerable time and effort in learning about outdated technology, without providing the return on your investment that a new machine could—and the difference in price between an old machine and a new one may not be as great as you might expect. If you choose to buy a used machine, seek guidance from someone who is knowledgeable about computers before you make a deal.

Two major manufacturers have dominated the personal computer market: The Apple Corporation and IBM. The cost of their machines remained relatively high until the IBM compatibles (or "clones") began to appear. Assembled by a variety of companies, these clones generally sold for much less than regular IBM PCs, enabling many more people to purchase personal computers. Apple did not experience such competition because it did not allow others to clone its operating system. Consequently, there was not much economic pressure to lower the prices of the early Apple computers or the later Macintosh machines.

Constantly changing computer technology and the increasing power of new generations of computer chips can confuse potential buyers. However, any of the newer machines on the market should serve your needs for several years.

Internal Components

All personal computers include some common components that you need to become familiar with before you buy. Although these components—the CPU, operating system, and memory—come with each computer, differences in their design can make a significant difference in the operation and performance of your system.

CPU

The personal computer consists of a variety of components collectively termed "hardware." One obvious component is the computer case (or "box"); within the case is an even more important component: The central processing unit (CPU), a silicon chip that is the heart of the computer. All other paraphernalia—the power supply, monitor, keyboard, disk drives, modem, and so on—are useless without it.

Operating System

A computer's operating system (OS) is the master program that enables the software to communicate with the hardware. Technically, the OS is software, not hardware, because it is installed on the computer's hard disk via diskettes. However, personal computers must have an operating system to function, and usually an OS has already been installed when you purchase the computer's hardware. Therefore, we will refer to the OS as a hardware component.

The basic PC operating system, disk operating system (DOS), is character-based: To make the computer perform tasks, you must enter instructions, or commands, character by character. If you make an error in entering a command—for example, if you misspell a word, insert an extra space, or omit a colon (:)—the only outcome is a message saying that the computer does not recognize the command. This can be very frustrating, especially for beginners who don't know what they've done wrong.

The Macintosh operating system is easier to set up than the PC and has a more friendly graphical user interface (GUI, pronounced "gooey")—that is, the items you see on your screen and the methods you use to access information are more self-explanatory and require less training. The Macintosh uses a "mouse," a palm-sized accessory that sits next to the computer and enables you to move an on-screen pointer to access the electronic tools you need. On the mouse is a button that you click when you have positioned the pointer on a particular tool (or icon). As you click, the computer performs the appropriate function.

Within the past several years, operating systems that look and feel similar to the Macintosh GUI have been developed for the PC: IBM has OS/2, and Microsoft has Windows. Through Microsoft's effective advertising campaigns, Windows has become the most popular operating system available. Most new PCs come with Windows installed.

Memory

Personal computers have two internal forms of storage, or memory: Hard disk memory and random access memory (RAM). As you compare computer packages, you should consider the amount of both types of memory included with each system. (However, you can buy memory separately and install it in the computer if you find you need more.)

• **Hard disk:** The information you enter in the computer is saved on a circular disk, which is coated with a material containing magnetic particles, similar to that used on audio and video tapes. A computer comes with a hard disk and one or more diskette drives. The hard disk is hardware inside the computer that stores a great deal of information including the computer's OS (for example, DOS, Windows, or Macintosh), the software applications, and much of the data you enter. The space for this storage is measured in units called bytes and grouped in increments of one million, called megabytes (MB). One thousand MB is a gigabyte (GB). Because most major software programs require a great deal of storage space, and because the cost of such space continues to decline, most new computers offer a minimum of 300MB of hard disk space, and machines with a gigabyte or more are common.

• **RAM:** The primary purpose of RAM is to store application and computer operating information. RAM also stores some of the data that you enter or retrieve from disks. Unlike data stored on disks, data stored in RAM is lost when you turn off the machine. If the power goes out in the middle of a project, the data you have entered will be lost, unless you have saved it to a disk. Although many applications offer you the option of saving your work automatically at set intervals (for example, every 10 minutes), you should cultivate the habit of manually saving your work frequently during computer sessions.

RAM comes in increments of 4MB. When you purchase a personal computer, be sure your new system has a minimum of 8MB of RAM. Your computer will run graphics applications faster and more efficiently with more RAM, so have as much RAM installed on the machine as you can afford. To take full advantage of today's computer operating systems (such as Windows 3.1, Windows 95, OS/2, and Macintosh System 7.5) and the software applications designed to run on these systems, you need at least 16MB of RAM.

Peripheral Components

Peripherals are external pieces that you can purchase to enhance the performance of your computer. Some, such as keyboards and monitors, are mandatory if you wish to use the computer, and computer packages usually include them. Other peripherals, such as modems and scanners, are optional; you should purchase them only if you need their specific functionality.

Keyboards

Most computer keyboards have the letter, number, and shift keys in the standard typewriter positions, plus function keys (labeled F1, F2, and so on) at the top of the keyboard, arrow keys on the right of the character keys, and a number pad on the far right. Various other keys, such as the Control, Option, and Delete keys, perform specific functions that help you manipulate information on the computer screen.

You will spend a great deal of time using the keyboard, so get one that feels comfortable to you. Try several—some companies offer ergonomic keyboards designed to fit human hands more naturally. If everything about a computer package appeals to you except the keyboard, consider purchasing one separately.

Monitors

The monitor is one of the most important components of your computer system. Because you spend so much time staring at it, you should look at several and purchase one that is comfortable to view. Most computer packages include color monitors; however, monochrome (black and white) monitors are also available. You'll find considerable variation between brands, and you'll make a worthwhile investment by spending a little more money to get a better quality monitor.

Make sure the monitor you are considering functions well with GUIs such as Windows; VGA or Super VGA (SVGA) monitors, with a screen size of fifteen inches or greater, are recommended. Also, pay attention to the dot pitch number (usually .39 or .28)—the smaller the number, the sharper the image. To reduce eyestrain, make sure you choose a non-interlaced monitor; interlaced monitors have a barely visible "flicker" resulting from the way their screens are scanned to produce images. Finally, although the health effects of electromagnetic radiation (EMR) are still being debated, you should purchase a monitor that meets Swedish MPR standards for low radiation if you are concerned about EMR.

Disks

In addition to the hard disk, computers generally use two other types of portable disks: Diskettes and compact disks (CDs). Personal computers come with one or more diskette drives, and newer models include a CD-ROM drive as well. Diskettes and CDs are portable, meaning you can easily take them out of one machine and insert them in another.

- **Diskettes:** Diskettes are 3.5-inch or 5.25-inch square plastic disks that you can remove from your computer and carry in your pocket, purse, or binder. (The larger diskettes are obsolete, however, and most new computers will accept only the smaller diskettes.) Just as file folders enable you to carry papers from one office to another, diskettes enable you to carry electronically stored information from one computer to another.

- **CD-ROM (Compact Disk-Read-Only Memory):** CDs are specially constructed plastic disks that are very durable and store much more information than diskettes. You cannot enter that information yourself; it comes on the CD (hence ROM, for Read-Only Memory).

CD-ROMs have several attractive features that make the purchase of a CD-ROM drive worth considering. First, CD-ROMs offer the least expensive way to publish—and therefore to purchase—large amounts of data. Furthermore, it enables you to make far more efficient use of data than any other medium: With electronic indexing, you can perform searches in seconds that might require months of research in printed sources. Also, installing software applications from CD-ROM to your hard disk drive is much faster and less tedious than installing them from diskettes. Finally, because the CD-ROM cannot be overwritten, it is a more secure medium than diskettes for your valuable applications.

CD-ROM technology is quite reliable, and the cost for a basic drive has become relatively inexpensive. The cost of individual CDs also continues to decline as titles continue to multiply. (See Chapter 12 for more information on CD-ROM sources.)

Printers

The type of printer you should purchase depends on your budget and the quality of output you want. Laser printers occupy the top end of the price and quality scale, followed by ink jet and finally dot-matrix printers. Color printers are also available, but they are expensive and unnecessary for most genealogists. See Pence's *Computer Genealogy* for a detailed explanation of the variety and functionality of printers.

Modems

The ability to use your computer and telephone line to access information at distant locations and to communicate with other genealogists could be the most important reason for investing in a computer. However, you need a modem (a device used to connect a computer to a telephone line) and telecommunications software to perform such tasks. (Many modems come with basic software.) Telecommunications and modems are described in more detail in Chapter 11.

Scanners

A scanner is a computer accessory that digitizes an image so a computer can read it. In other words, scanners make photocopies and send them to computer monitors. Scanners enable you to electronically store pictures of ancestors, maps, and source documents and link them to text. You can use a scanner with many software applications; some even offer scanning as a standard feature.

After you've scanned typed or typeset pages, you can use optical character recognition (OCR) software to change the image into manipulable text so that you can edit documents without retyping them. At present, however, OCR software is not so much a serious genealogical computing tool as it is an expensive, advanced toy.

Getting Help With Computer Issues

Everyone needs help with computer-related problems from time to time. In addition to getting help from books and friends, you can also obtain assistance from individuals in the hundreds of computer interest groups (CIGs) worldwide. You can find user groups for PC, Macintosh, genealogy, specific software applications, and myriad other topics. Such groups can be a great bargain to both novice and expert computer users because they offer personalized help, discounted equipment and supplies, newsletters, vendor information, club libraries of books and applications, member rosters, and much more.

The Computer Shopper, a periodical from Coastal Associates Publishing, provides a current (albeit incomplete) listing of local CIGs every other month. For a complete and accurate list, you can download George Archer' consolidated list of CIGs from a FidoNet bulletin board system (BBS) or from the Internet at http://genealogy.org//NGS. This is the address for the National Genealogical Society (NGS). Once you have accessed this site, you can select the CIG list (or a variety of other documents) from a menu.

Many CIGs are available on BBSs and the Internet. As you make hardware and software purchasing decisions, you can query these CIGs for users' opinions of various systems and applications. (See Chapter 11 for details about accessing information on the Internet.)

Bibliography

Pence, R.A., ed. *Computer Genealogy*. Salt Lake City, UT: Ancestry, 1991.

The Computer Shopper, monthly periodical. New York, NY: Coastal Associates Publishing.

Chapter 10

Computer Software

When we published our first book in 1984, our motto was, "Find the software you like, then buy hardware to run it." This adage still holds true. Similarly, as you look at genealogy applications, remember that each succeeding software generation requires more memory, speed, and disk space than the last, so you should obtain the most powerful computer system you can afford.

For a software application to run, it must be compatible with the computer's operating system (OS). For example, if your computer's OS is Windows, you cannot use a software application that is written for Macintosh only; you must run the Windows version of that application. Many software developers write applications for multiple OSs, but if you know you want to use a particular application, make sure it is written for the OS that you plan to run on your computer. (See Chapter 9 for more information on operating systems.)

Because Microsoft Windows and Windows 95 use DOS code (DOS was the first OS designed for IBM computers and their clones), generally you can still use your older DOS applications after you've migrated to Windows. In addition, newer operating systems, such as Windows 95 and OS/2, incorporate many of the smaller utility applications for compression and disk maintenance, so you don't have to purchase them separately.

When you consider software, you should generally think of the process in terms of "subscribing to" an application rather than "buying" it: Most quality software is enhanced and updated continually, and when you purchase one version, companies usually offer upgraded versions to you at relatively inexpensive prices. If your original software choice is good, you can expect to stick with it through several upgrades before switching to something newer and better.

Be cautious about upgrading to new software and even to newer versions of existing software. New applications often have problems (or "bugs"), so you should wait for them to be tested in the marketplace before you upgrade. Software companies commonly release minor upgrades that correct bugs—for example, the major release of an application might be version 6.0, and the debugged release, version 6.0a or 6.1. To be safe when you do purchase upgrades, you should save your old application and data.

Choosing Genealogy Software

You'll probably need three types of software: a word processor, which simplifies the writing process and can help you keep updated research agendas and summary sheets, write letters, and even publish a finished genealogy; a telecommunications application (discussed in Chapter 11); and a genealogy application. Genealogy software can help you gather, organize, and research your data.

General Criteria

You may need to try several genealogy packages before you find one that satisfies your needs. Before you purchase a genealogy application, be sure it meets the following criteria:

- Handles large numbers of linked names reliably, without corrupting data or crashing

- Enables downloading of large amounts of data

- Allows you to edit records easily, define fields, and attach unlimited notes

- Offers good vendor support, meaning that the maker of the software package will help you resolve any problem you may encounter with it

- Provides an acceptable strategy for handling name variations

- Includes GEDCOM compatibility, so you can download data from other sources as GEDCOM files (Some genealogists use more than one GEDCOM-compatible genealogy application so that they can use the best features of each)

- Displays sorted lists for most fields

- Displays and prints standard forms (family group and pedigree charts, ahnentafels, and so on)

- Links events with source documents

- Searches on names, places, dates, and notes

- Finds first, middle, and last names, as well as portions of names

- Generates statistical information from your database (frequency of a particular name, average age at marriage, and so on)

- Feels good to *you*, since you will spend hours using it

Specific Features

If the application meets the above criteria, begin looking at the specific tasks you want to accomplish. For instance, several years ago we wanted to build an inclusive pedigree-linked database for our U.S. colonial-era research. We chose an application called Brother's Keeper because it offered the features we needed to accomplish our task with greater ease and efficiency. Some of the most valuable features included the following:

* **Wildcard searching:** This feature enables you to evaluate previously collected information about any surname and locate possible connections between families in which unusual first names appear. For instance, by entering "? Jones," you can view a list of every Jones in the database, alphabetically by first name. By entering "Herbert ?" you can view a list of every person whose first name was Herbert, alphabetically by last name.

* **Macros:** Macro capability enables you to instruct the computer to automate a particular task when you press a specific key. Recording macros saves you the trouble of entering the same name, location, or source description repeatedly—instead, you press one key that enters the information for you. For example, we have programmed keys to enter phrases such as "unproved, but likely," and "unproved, but possible." With one keystroke, we can place these phrases next to relationships that are based on circumstantial evidence.

* **Complete source citation:** With complete source citation, each event field is linked to a field in which you can identify the source of the information. Completing the source field will help you research thoroughly and record data accurately.

* **Screening for duplicates:** This feature enables you to compare information for all individuals in your database with the same name. Doing so helps you avoid duplication (and often considerable confusion).

* **Simple revision of data:** This feature makes creating and editing records easy. You can add a new record or access an existing one simply by entering a name. Similarly, revising records is simple: You can change the position of a name in the family structure; delete a name (from a marriage, a family, or the entire database); change the order of marriages or children; and correct (throughout the database, if desired) dates, places, or sources. (Brother's Keeper also provides a handy footnote feature that helps you access any amount of ASCII-formatted data from your database.)

- **Customizable fields:** With customizable fields, you can customize all fields on the screen (except name, birth, and death) to suit your needs.

Learning About Genealogy Software

You can read about genealogy applications in various publications such as *Genealogical Computing*, a quarterly journal from Ancestry Incorporated. Online sources—especially bulletin boards, electronic mail (e-mail) groups, and newsgroups—are probably the best way to learn about the quality and capabilities of various software applications. (See Chapter 11 for more information about online services.)

Shareware

We've become familiar with several good genealogy applications, including Brother's Keeper and Family Scrapbook, by downloading them as shareware. Shareware is software that you can try before you buy: You can obtain a free copy from a computer interest group (CIG), bulletin board system (BBS), commercial online service provider, the Internet, or shareware sources advertised in magazines. You can use the application for a time; if you like it enough to keep using it, you must pay for it. Registration information is usually included in a file accompanying the application.

Commercial Software

Some commercial applications are less expensive than shareware. For instance, you can purchase Personal Ancestral File (PAF), a widely used genealogy software package developed by the Family History Department of The Church of Jesus Christ of Latter-day Saints (the LDS church), for just $35 in both PC and Macintosh versions. You can try PAF at many LDS family history centers (see Chapter 4) and order it through any of them. Even if you don't own a computer, you can visit an LDS family history center and automate your data using a computer with PAF installed. PAF is compatible with—but not the same as—an important CD-ROM collection issued by the LDS church called Ancestral File (discussed in Chapter 4).

GEDCOM

GEDCOM is an application that translates genealogical data into a standardized exchange format. GEDCOM, which is included in PAF, was developed to enable large-scale input of family data into Ancestral File through the personal computer. Since the introduction of GEDCOM several years ago, portions of it have been incorporated into many other genealogy applications—you can obtain an updated list of GEDCOM-compatible software packages from the LDS Family History Department by writing to the following address:

Ancestral File Operations Unit
50 East North Temple Street
Salt Lake City, UT 84150

GEDCOM extracts information from a database and puts it into a specially tagged format that allows you to move data into or out of any application that recognizes the GEDCOM format. The application uses symbols to represent records and their links to other records. In the example shown below, the zero (0) indicates the beginning of a new individual record, number I414. The next hierarchy of information is indicated by the number 1. Each field with a number 2 corresponds to the number 1 field that precedes it—for example, 16 FEB 1842 (on the fifth line) is the date of christening (CHR) for John William Costello.

```
0 @I414@ INDI
1 NAME  John William /Costello/
1 SEX   M
1 CHR
2 DATE  16 FEB 1842
2 PLAC  Duagh,Kerry,Ireland
1 DEAT
2 DATE  1918
2 PLAC  2nd St S.W.,Calgary,Alberta,Canada
1 BURI
2 DATE  1918
2 PLAC  StMarysCemetery,Calgary,Alberta,Canada
1 FAMS  @F213@
1 FAMC  @F92@
```

The last two lines of this record provide links to two other Individual records: FAMS @F213@ is for Costello's spouse, and FAMC @F92@ is for his child.

GEDCOM compatibility has played an important role in computer genealogy because it allows researchers to export data from one application to another and obviates the need to re-enter data. In addition, GEDCOM has encouraged competition between software developers: Users who are not satisfied with one application can easily switch to another without worrying about software compatibility. This forces developers to continually improve and enhance their software packages. Unfortunately, different applications use different versions of GEDCOM (now on its fifth revision). Consequently, not all GEDCOM-compatible applications are fully compatible with one another, so you may lose some data when you transfer it between applications.

Some researchers criticize the current GEDCOM version for its tight structure—they claim it lacks the flexibility required for genealogical data. However, the LDS church, which sets the standard for genealogical research and software, feels that greater structure is needed for data to be integrated with the church's huge data files. While the conflict may cause some software developers to discontinue their support for GEDCOM, there are still reasons for limiting your consideration of genealogy software to only those programs that are compatible with GEDCOM. By doing so, you will be able to share your data with others, both directly and through Ancestral File, and you will be able to upgrade easily to better software packages as they become available.

Bibliography

Archer, George. *Archer's Directory of Genealogical Software*. Bowie, MD: Heritage Books, 1993. Less detailed than Przecha and Lowrey's guide, but comprehensive: Contains information for all pre-1993 genealogy applications. Includes purchasing information for each package.

Computers in Genealogy, published quarterly. London, UK: Society of Genealogists. Contains some interesting articles for genealogists, and includes software reviews.

Genealogical Computing, published quarterly. Salt Lake City, UT: Ancestry. To subscribe, write P.O. Box 476, Salt Lake City, UT 84110.

Przecha, Donna, and Joan Lowrey. *Guide to Genealogical Software*. Baltimore, MD: Genealogical Publishing Co., 1993. Supplies detailed information for about thirty-five of the most popular pre-1993 genealogy applications.

Chapter 11

Telecommunications

The word *telecommunications* describes the exchange of information through electronic means. For genealogists, these means generally include a telephone line, modem, facsimile machine (fax), and computer. Using current computer telecommunications technology, you can send a message or inquiry to a single individual or thousands of people. Furthermore, you'll find an abundance of software, news articles, information files, bibliographies, databases, and other resources by using electronic bulletin boards and networks.

For the home computer user, telecommunications require a personal computer, a telecommunications application, a modem, and a telephone line. Linking them is not difficult. You don't need to know how all the components work; you just need to know that a modem and a telecommunications program loaded on the computer make it all happen.

Modems

A modem is a device connected to the computer that allows it to communicate with another computer in the same way the telephone allows you to talk with another person. The word *modem* is derived from MOdulate and DEModulate, terms that describe changes in an electrical signal. There are two types of modems: An internal modem is installed inside the computer; an external modem is housed in a small box that you connect to the computer. The following terms are important in modem technology:

- **bps:** An abbreviation of *bits per second*, used to describe the speed at which the computer can send and receive information through a modem.

- **Baud:** Another way of describing the speed at which information can be sent or received through a modem. Baud is often used incorrectly instead of bps.

- **Port:** An outlet on a computer (usually on the back) that allows a modem, printer, or other device to exchange information with the computer's CPU. There are two basic types of ports: parallel and serial. A parallel port is used primarily to connect a printer to a computer. A serial port, or COM port, is used to connect a modem to a computer. Most computers have several COM ports (COM1, COM2, COM3, and so on); however, you will be primarily concerned with COM1 and COM2. Typically, one is used for the modem and the other for attaching the mouse. Regardless of whether you have an internal or external modem, you must assign one port to the modem.

Modems that send and receive data at rates as high as 14400 bps are now standard and relatively inexpensive. You can get a slower modem (2400 bps) at a lower price, but you should acquire a 14400 modem if you can afford it.

Telecommunications Software

Although the port enables you to make the physical connection between a modem and a computer, to function with the telephone line, a modem requires a software application so it can dial, send messages and files (upload), receive files (download), and perform other tasks.

Many modems come with telecommunications software, but the quality varies. Examine the documentation that comes with the software to determine whether it provides the functionality you need. Generally, software purchased separately includes more features and a friendlier interface (see Glossary).

Telecommunications software is available in both commercial and shareware versions; ask other users and software dealers for suggestions.

Electronic Bulletin Boards

Almost every community of computer enthusiasts has at least one local electronic bulletin board system (BBS). Depending on which services it provides, you can exchange electronic mail (e-mail), read bulletins, upload and download files, and participate in online discussions with other BBS members.

Local BBSs vary both in number and quality. The number depends on where you live, and the quality depends on the expertise and commitment of the system operator (sysop) who manages the BBS. Generally, local BBSs—which are free or very inexpensive to join—offer a convenient place to start online explorations. Many also offer worldwide telecommunication privileges.

Using Commercial Online Services

In addition to local BBSs, there are several commercial online services, including America Online (AOL), CompuServe, Delphi, GEnie, and Prodigy. These services require a monthly subscription fee, plus additional charges for some services. Many provide low-cost offline reader software that enables you to perform tasks such as composing and reading e-mail and preparing files for uploading before you go online, which can lower your monthly bill.

Genealogical interest groups or forums through which you can learn and exchange information are found in most of these commercial services, including all those named in the preceding paragraph. Such groups are usually run by volunteer hosts who function like sysops. With the growing popularity of the Internet and the intense competition within the telecommunications industry, some of these online services are losing membership. In general, the larger the membership, the better tool it is for genealogists. So if you decide to join one, make sure it is one that is growing, as well as offering good rates.

BBSs and large networks are becoming increasingly interconnected. For genealogists, the difference between a BBS and a network is one of power and scope. A large network (for example, the Internet) enables you to communicate with many more people and is faster than a BBS because of the more direct nature of the communication. With many BBSs and most networks, you can communicate in the following ways:

- Send and receive e-mail or echoed messages

- Upload and download files (text, applications, graphics)

- Access special interest groups or news groups

The networks (freenets, the Internet, and so on) allow you to access distant computers that house excellent resources—for example, the Library of Congress book catalog.

Connecting and Quitting

To connect to a BBS, use the dialing directory or menu provided by the telecommunications software you use. Good software allows you to create a list, or directory, of commonly called numbers. Associated with the number, you need to type a line that looks something like this: 14400, N,8,1. Translated, the entry means 14,400 bps, no parity checking, 8 data bits, and 1 stop bit. The information required depends on the BBS. When you exchange information through a modem, the data is sent in packets of bits (electrical pulses). A "parity" bit indicates what type of basic error checking will be done on the information you are sending or receiving. A "stop" bit marks the end of each packet.

Once connected to a BBS, you are prompted to enter your name and a password. Give some thought to the password; a common or easily decoded password may allow someone else to access your account. It's a good idea to mix upper- and lower-case letters, numerals, and/or nonalphabetic characters in your password (for example, exTra$Man), or to use an uncommon word or name that bears no relation to genealogical or online activities. Make sure you remember the password! After your initial access of a BBS, you will log on by entering your name or some identification code provided by the BBS, and your password.

As a new user, you will be instructed on how to join the BBS, and how to explore it before you join. Almost all BBSs use a series of menus from which you can choose, for example:

* A—News and bulletins pertaining to the board

* B—User groups

* C—Files you can download

* G—Goodbye or Logoff

* H—Help

To exit the BBS (called logging off or out), look for instructions, which are usually provided on the first screen you see after you log on. If problems occur that keep you from following the proper etiquette for leaving a board, just hang up as described in the documentation for your telecommunications software to avoid unnecessary phone charges.

Accessing System Operator (Sysop) Help

There are often different levels of access on a BBS. New users may be restricted in terms of the time they may spend in the BBS or the number of files they may download. Full access usually requires membership registration, which normally consists of answering a few questions and selecting a password. The sysop of the BBS wants to know something about you before giving you extensive privileges.

Even boards that charge usually allow newcomers to explore or browse their holdings, and often to download the list of available files. We recommend capturing or logging to a file your entire initial exploring session (follow the instructions for downloading in the documentation for your telecommunications application). When you review the session, you can determine whether you want to register.

Be respectful of sysops; they allow you to use the system and provide answers to your questions—and you'll have many when you begin online exploration. Many boards have a menu choice called FAQ (frequently asked questions), or some other instructional area, that you can access if you have questions. If, after thoroughly reviewing the board's contents, you can't find the answers you need, choose the menu option that allows you to send messages and questions to the sysop.

Joining a Discussion Group

Most large BBSs have discussion groups, where members with similar interests can exchange information. These groups are also called conferences, special interest groups (SIGs), echoes, forums, message areas, folders, areas, subboards, or newsgroups. Some are devoted to genealogy, and thousands are devoted to other subjects. Nongenealogical groups that focus on computer software and hardware, history, geography, and culture may help your research indirectly. The information available through discussion groups is comparable to—but usually more current than—the information you might read in a newsletter.

It's easy to join a discussion group. Some are live, meaning that you can exchange information with others who are connected to the BBS at the same time as you are. Most, however, exchange all messages that are sent to the group so you can read and respond to any message at your convenience.

Many genealogical conferences offer software applications, utilities, and text files that members can download. You can obtain many genealogy shareware packages this way.

Locating a Local Bulletin Board

The best way to find BBSs in your area is to dial a large genealogy BBS, such as ROOTS(SF!) in San Francisco (415-584-0697), Ancestry in Lake Placid, Florida (813-471-0552), or the popular National Genealogical Society BBS near Washington, D.C. (703-528-2612), and download or search the file containing the most current version of *Dick Pence's Consolidated List of Genealogy Bulletin Boards*. This frequently updated catalog includes alphabetical listings (by state, then city) of more than eight hundred active FidoNet boards that carry genealogical information. Expect overlap between boards; most pick up and echo files and messages from the others.

You may also find BBSs available in your area by contacting local computer stores or computer user groups, or consulting the following publications:

- *The Computer Shopper:* A monthly publication that provides a current (though probably incomplete) list of BBSs in every other issue. Entries are listed alphabetically by state, then area code. Information includes fees, brief descriptions of contents, date established, and technical specifications for connecting.

- *Modem USA: Low-Cost and Free Online Sources:* A book that lists local BBSs and their topics by state. It also contains chapters that discuss libraries, books, computers, and genealogy. Some two hundred genealogy

File   Edit   Mailbox   Message   Transfer   Special   Window   Help

		In	

| 34/165K/46K | | | | | | |

R	Cyril Taylor	09:04 AM 5/28/95	3	Cambria County, PA
	Nuchar@aol.com	12:01 AM 6/6/95	1	Irish in Blair Co.
R	RDMonahan@aol.co	08:27 AM 6/9/95	3	Re: Irish in Blair & Cambria ...
	Timothy Noonan	08:13 PM 6/10/95	6	Wisconsin Indexes
	Barbara Bruxvoor	04:54 PM 7/13/95	3	Re: California Wagon Train Lists price?
	Frank O'Donnell	08:30 PM 7/24/95	3	Catholic records
	Caryl Gray	03:43 PM 7/25/95	2	Fall Planner
	Eileen Hitchingh	04:20 PM 7/26/95	2	Meeting Maker (fwd)
●	John Stemmer	06:18 PM 7/26/95	3	Signature Files and Area Codes
●	Jeannie Vaughan	07:40 PM 7/26/95	3	Re: subsets of GEDCOM files (ex family Tree M
●	Michelle Mason	09:31 PM 7/26/95	2	Re: research
●	Automatic digest	08:40 PM 7/26/95	45	ROOTS: ROOTS-L Digest - 26 Jul 1995 - Special
●	Steven R. Moen	11:44 AM 7/26/95	2	TMG: WOW!!!!
●	Peter Scott	06:08 PM 7/26/95	2	Vacation Time for the moderator
●	Jane Dundas Libr	10:01 PM 7/26/95	2	PUBLIB: info. on search engines?
●	Jean Armour Poll	10:13 PM 7/26/95	4	PUBLIB: NEW: MEDIALIB - Library Media List
●	Heather Campbell	10:13 PM 7/26/95	3	PUBLIB: ?Library Web Pages
●	Michael Andersso	04:14 PM 7/26/95	3	CHANGE: SWEDE-L has moved
●	Denis Beauregard	10:28 PM 7/26/95	2	Re: subsets of GEDCOM files (ex family Tree M
●	Denis Beauregard	11:06 PM 7/26/95	3	Re: subsets of GEDCOM files (ex family Tree M
●	Karen Ann Coffey	11:17 PM 7/26/95	4	AOL Users...(Ignore all others)
●	Tim Doyle	07:58 PM 7/26/95	2	TMG: Re: Bug in printing reports and a work-a
●	Clarice Jane Sny	12:28 AM 7/27/95	2	Re: subsets of GEDCOM files (...
●	Charlie Towne	05:34 PM 7/26/95	3	TMG: Re: Bug in printing reports and a work-a
●	Automatic digest	12:07 AM 7/27/95	22	ROOTS: ROOTS-L Digest - 26 Jul 1995
●	Automatic digest	12:00 AM 7/27/95	22	WINNT-L Digest - 26 Jul 1995
●	hbladml@uconnvm.	10:03 PM 7/26/95	2	TMG: Re: Tag: Land gift/purchase

**Figure 11-1. Members of Discussion Groups Can Read and Reply to
Any Message That Has Been Posted to the Group**

BBSs are listed in the latest edition, as well as valuable information on
several local boards that offer Internet access. The book costs $19.95,
including shipping. To order, call 202-291-8941, or write to the following
address:

Allium Press
P.O. Box 5752-39
Takoma Park, MD 20913-5752

• **Various periodicals:** Many other magazines also give information about
BBSs and other online services—*Board Watch, Connect, Online Access,
Online, Information Today, PC Computing, PC Novice, MacWorld,* and
PC Magazine are a few. These periodicals are written for various
audiences, from novice computer users to telecommunications experts.

Networks

In the world of telecommunications, *network* refers to the electronic linking of
computers to create a web of connections with simple to extraordinarily
complex structure. Networks fall into two basic categories: local area networks
(LANs) and wide area networks (WANs). A LAN is generally a network set

up for an office, enabling computers to share information and software applications. Computer terminals are linked by cables to one or more central computers called mainframes or servers. A WAN is a network composed of any combination of LANs, BBSs, and remote computers (such as home systems). Computers are linked through telephone lines and, if the WAN spans large distances, by satellite.

LANs and WANs can be connected to each other through special devices called routers to form large internetworks. FidoNet, the Internet, and freenets are examples of internetworks.

FidoNet

FidoNet is an international network of BBSs with tens of thousands of public and private nodes (computers connected to a network). It boasts more than one million users, including many in less-developed countries. In the U.S., numerous local BBSs belong to FidoNet, which carries many conferences (frequently called *echoes*), including approximately two dozen genealogical conferences. Each BBS on the FidoNet chooses which echoes to carry.

Several hundred new messages from the U.S. and abroad may be posted daily on the FidoNet genealogy echo, but few articles are truly worth reading. Offline reader software can bundle messages so you can download them as a single file to reduce long-distance charges. Good offline readers allow key word searching to help you quickly find the messages that interest you. Ask the BBS sysop to suggest a reader—not all BBSs support all readers.

The Internet

The Internet is an ever-growing "network of networks." It connects users in universities, corporations, government agencies, and other organizations in most of the developed world. The Internet includes or provides access to many other networks.

In August 1991, 500,000 host computers were linked to the Internet. By the end of 1993, the number exceeded 2 million, and today experts estimate that 20 million to 30 million users are connected. The development of friendly graphical user interfaces (GUIs)—many of them free or very inexpensive—has transformed the Internet from a network used only by technically trained researchers into a mainstream information source. Software can help you read and manage e-mail, browse, transfer files, search for specific information, read and manage newsgroup discussions, find other users, connect to online library catalogs, and more.

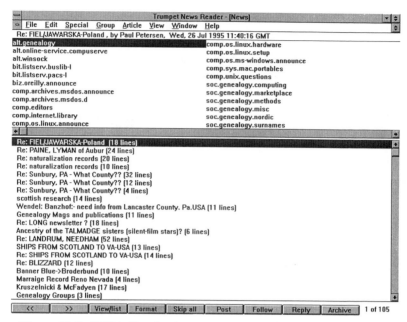

Figure 11-2. Offline Reader Software Such as Trumpet News Reader Can Bundle Messages for Downloading

The Internet offers a plethora of information on genealogy as well as related subjects, such as geography, culture, and history. With links in more than two hundred countries, the Internet provides unrivaled opportunities for a worldwide exchange of ideas and information.

Access

Practically anyone with a computer can access the Internet. You can pay for full access—which allows you to use the World Wide Web (WWW), e-mail, newsgroups, File Transfer Protocol (FTP), and remote login (Telnet)—or choose only the services you need. Increasing numbers of public libraries, businesses, and educational institutions are gaining full or partial access to the Internet. In addition, many BBSs and commercial systems have begun to offer Internet services.

You can access most freenets and many commercial online services from the Internet. You can also search for information in databases that contain magazine articles, and commercial providers will mail or fax the article to you for a fee. For example, the CARL system in Colorado allows potential

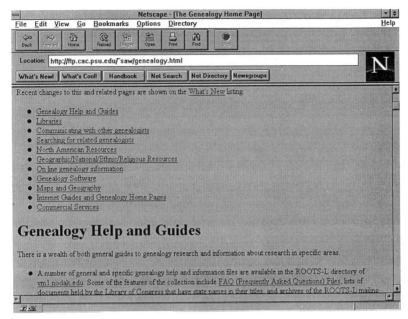

Figure 11-3. The Genealogy Homepage on the World Wide Web

customers to search its database of periodical articles free (telnet database.carl.org).

World Wide Web

One of the fastest-growing segments of the Internet is called the World Wide Web (WWW). It enables you to click on key words and icons to move directly from one source of information to another. In addition to its ease-of-use, the WWW offers visual appeal: A page on the Web can be as attractive as any page layout in a magazine. If you conduct a key word search on *genealogy*, you'll find WWW pages for numerous national and state archives, libraries, genealogical societies, and myriad genealogical sources that provide indexes to census records and other information.

E-mail

With electronic mail, or e-mail, you can exchange messages with network users throughout the world using electronic addresses. An example of an address on the Internet is johndoe@vtvm1.cc.vt.edu. The pieces of the address signify the following:

- **johndoe:** The logon user ID

- **vtvml:** Computer name

- **cc:** Computing center

- **vt:** Domain name (for example, Virginia Tech)

- **edu:** Type of facility (edu = educational)

You do not need direct Internet access to use the Internet's globe-spanning e-mail capacity: Most BBSs and networks provide e-mail service. Increasing numbers of small BBSs, along with most commercial providers, trade e-mail with the Internet, but some have file size limits or extra charges for use beyond a specified time limit.

E-mail gives you quick access to expertise throughout the world and is less expensive than regular postal service. Using e-mail and Internet connections, we quickly received guidance for some topics in this book from experts as far away as South Africa. Also, by tracking e-mail messages in some genealogy newsgroups, we have found distant relatives with whom we have exchanged genealogical information.

Newsgroups
Newsgroups are electronic collections of articles, notes, and messages between individuals with common interests. On the Internet, you can find many genealogy newsgroups, including the following:

- soc.genealogy.misc

- soc.genealogy.computing

- soc.genealogy.methods

- soc.genealogy.surnames

- soc.genealogy.french

- soc.genealogy.german

- soc.genealogy.jewish

As with messages posted to FidoNet, you can use offline reader software to manage information in newsgroups and keep your costs down. The Internet provider you use controls which newsgroups you can access; however, you can browse most newsgroups by using Telnet. Some newer readers not only can provide access to all available groups at your site, they can also alert you when new groups come online (which is almost daily).

FTP

File Transfer Protocol (FTP) software enables you to transfer files from other computers on the Internet to your desktop. Many sites allow you to log in to their computers by using the word "anonymous" as your user name and your Internet address as a password. (You receive an Internet address when you join an organization that offers Internet access.)

Telnet

Telnet enables you to access a computer on the Internet directly, as if your keyboard were connected to that computer, to access information. As with FTP, special software is required to conduct a Telnet session. Telnet is most frequently used to access Online Public Access Catalogs (OPACs), online databases, and freenets.

Freenets

Freenets are grassroots services connected to the Internet that offer networking to their communities free of charge—local library systems often provide freenet access. Anyone is welcome to register and use their services. If you can access a freenet locally, you aren't required to pay long-distance telephone rates.

The first—and largest—freenet was established in Cleveland, Ohio; you can access it at telnet freenets-in-a.cwru.edu or by dialing 216-368-3888. It offers e-mail, usenet groups, FidoNet genealogy echoes, and its own genealogy SIG known as Roots. Between 1986 and 1989, five freenets were formed in cities in Ohio and Illinois. Subsequently, many others have sprung up throughout the U.S. and Canada.

Networks and Genealogical Research

Computer networks provide better results for some types of research than for other types. Generally, networking will help you accomplish the following tasks successfully:

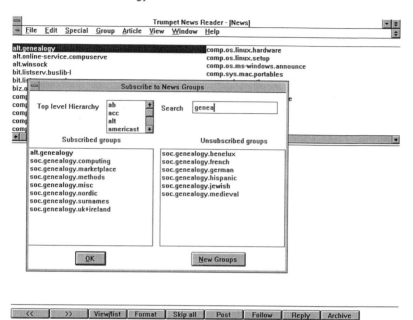

**Figure 11-4. You Can Subscribe to Many Genealogy Newsgroups on
the Internet**

- Access shareware and obtain user opinions about software

- Pinpoint obscure geographical locations

- Locate library books that discuss ancestral names

- Gain historical background information

- Learn details about distant record centers

- Access computerized records that can help your research

Until quite recently, networking was only a marginally successful method of
finding other researchers interested in your family names. But with the
expansion of the Internet, your chances of successfully locating relatives who
are doing research keep increasing. Simply post and look for your names of
interest in the appropriate newsgroups. You may also want to upload your
ancestral names into a FidoNet TinyTafel (TT) file, which is a specially
formatted, single surname line that you can upload to a BBS that participates
in the Tafel Matching System (TMS). The file is added to a TT archive and
matched to surnames with a similar spelling or Soundex code (see Appendix
A) in other archive sites. When the process is complete, you can download a

report that contains the matching TTs, along with the names and addresses of their submitters.

Another useful online service is database matching. Many online organizations will allow you to upload databases, which are then compared to the other databases in that organization. You are alerted of potential matches. The Silicon Valley PAF Users Group (SVPAFUG) has such a system. You can obtain instructions for participation from the group's WWW homepage: http://www.rahul.net/svpafug.

In March 1996, Brøderbund Software, which sells a genealogy application called Family Tree Maker and a collection of genealogy CD-ROMs (see Chapter 12), published its FamilyFinder index to a Web page on the Internet (www.familytreemaker.com). The index lists about 118 million names from the company's CD-ROM collection. As it publishes new CDs, Brøderbund plans to update the index.

The Future of Networking

Networking is the fastest-growing segment of the computer industry, and it offers great opportunities for genealogists. In the future, individual databases will be combined at the Internet level into one all-encompassing, dynamic, electronic database called the GenWeb. This network, the brainchild of Gary Hoffmann of the Computer Genealogy Society of San Diego, will enable you to share notes and sources, pinpoint errors, and link data for each ancestor to every other database on the Internet that contains data for that individual. The possibilities of such a network are fantastic—the afterword of this book discusses the reasons why the GenWeb has greater potential to advance genealogy than any other development since the advent of computers.

Chapter 12

CD-ROM Sources

CD-ROM publishing is growing explosively: In 1988 there were eight titles on CD-ROM; by 1996, the number had risen to more than 13,000. CD-ROM players now sell for as little as $200, down from about $1,200 five years ago, and prices will probably continue to fall. CD-ROM mastering equipment has become so affordable that even small operations such as genealogical societies and family organizations will soon begin using this technology to store and distribute data. (Many valuable CD-ROMs have been published by the LDS church as part of its FamilySearch collection, discussed in Chapter 4.)

Library Reference Databases

CD-ROMs can aid your research significantly. Many have powerful search engines that can pick out specific items from vast quantities of data in seconds. We'll begin by considering some of the CD-ROMs you are likely to find during library research (aside from the phone CDs, which are discussed in Chapter 4):

- *Biography and Genealogy Master Index:* This index lists more than 8.5 million biographies (dating back to 1976) on more than 3 million people. Birth and death dates are provided for each name, and publication information is supplied for each biography.

- *Marquis's Who's Who:* This source includes all names listed in the series *Who's Who In . . .* , but offers more broad search criteria than just surname.

- *America: History and Life* and *Historical Abstracts:* Each of these titles provides abstracts and bibliographic citations of scholarly articles (from 2,100 journals each) on history and culture. The first collection covers the U.S. and Canada, and the second covers the rest of the world.

- *Dissertation Abstracts:* This collection contains summaries of doctoral dissertations from universities in the U.S. and Canada. The dissertations cover a variety of topics, including local and regional history.

Family Archives CD-ROMs from Banner Blue

Automated Archives was the first private company to specialize in CD-ROM genealogy. It developed its own searching software, known as GRS, and then published numerous CD-ROM data collections between the time it was incorporated in 1989 and both before and after becoming a division of Banner Blue software in 1994, which in turn became a division of Brøderbund software in 1995. Several helpful collections are now available.

The *Marriages Records Indexes* number more than 4 million. The first time we tried one of those disks, we felt like children on Christmas morning! We could search for all instances of a surname in one or more states, or even all recorded marriages for an entire county, often in less than a minute. This first marriage set includes five CDs covering parts of Alabama, Arkansas, Georgia, Illinois, Iowa, Kentucky, Louisiana, Maryland, Missouri, Mississippi, North and South Carolina, Ohio, Tennessee, Texas, and Virginia. These records were compiled by genealogists Nicholas and Dorothy Murray. The time period varies between areas, but it is mostly eighteenth and nineteenth century, with some seventeenth and twentieth century coverage. We have found the accuracy of this data to be quite good, although, as with almost any compiled source (especially those that include data from volunteer submissions or published family histories), there are some errors. And because only standard information (i.e., names of bride and groom, date and place of marriage) was abstracted, it is often worthwhile to check the record itself for additional facts that may have been included.

Another set of CDs for marriages through 1850 was more recently produced, based on the work of Liahona, Inc. There is some overlap, as this second marriage collection includes some of the same states as the first, namely: Arkansas, Iowa, Louisiana, Missouri, Oregon, Texas, Kentucky, Tennessee, Virginia, West Virginia, North Carolina, Illinois, Indiana, Georgia, Ohio, California, and Minnesota (just a smattering for these last two states; but Arizona, California, Idaho, and Nevada are now included in a good-sized marriage index that covers 1850-1951). New York marriages are found on yet another recently produced CD: *Selected Areas of New York, 1639-1916.*

Family trees compiled by genealogy research firms or individual researchers is another category of genealogy CD-ROMs. This includes a pedigree-linked database assembled by a now-defunct genealogical research company, United Ancestry, with some 750,000 pedigree-linked names, making it the second-largest linked database (after Ancestral File) in the world. Some lines go back to royal families, and thus date back to the thirteenth century and earlier.

(Recently Banner Blue has been releasing several *World Family Tree* CD-ROMs containing unmerged GEDCOM files from hundreds of family historians.)

The *U.S. Census Indexes* series was drawn from the AIS census index database and some other sources. When originally produced, these census indexes were arranged geographically, combining a few adjacent states onto one diskette. Since Brøderbund assumed ownership, those databases have been combined even more, so that the newer CDs are arranged by decades and cover the entire U.S., with the exception of areas which are missing censuses for that particular census decade. A particularly valuable census index for colonial America titled *Census Index: Colonial America, 1634-1790* is culled from tax lists and censuses from over a thousand pre-1790 sources. Besides the U.S. censuses, there is also one partial census index available for Ireland, *Census Index: Ireland, 1831-1841,* which includes county Londonderry in 1831 and county Cavan in 1841.

The highlight of the *Family History Collection* is "217 Genealogy Books" (most of these books now being out of print) for New England and the South. The CD format allows for every-word searching capability.

Some CDs now being produced use graphics imaging to reproduce images of the original handwritten records, while still offering regular CD-ROM search capabilities (talk about having your cake and eating it too!). One example is the *Military Records: U.S. Soldiers, 1784-1811* CD, indexing 21,000 volunteer soldiers who served in that era, as found in microfilmed National Archives records.

Most other imaged CDs reproduce books rather than microfilm. For example, the *Roll of Honor: Civil War Union Soldiers* is a CD version of the *Roll of Honor* volumes referenced in chapter 7. *The Complete Book of Emigrants, 1607-1776* CD is similarly based on a six-volume list of 140,000 English emigrants. (While by no means can it be considered "complete," it is a major resource we look forward to consulting.) Because the Family Tree Maker's Family Archive CD collection is expanding rather rapidly, check the "latest editions" section of their Web site regularly to keep yourself updated.

The Banner Blue division has also released an every-name index to its cumulative CD-ROM collection, now known as the *Family Finder Index.* There is some good news about this resource: The *Family Finder Index* generally allows researchers to learn in advance which of the published CDs contain names of interest to them; and the index includes well over 100 million names as we go to press. Unfortunately, there is also some bad news: The newer Windows-based software required by the *Family Finder Index* and by their recently reconfigured CD-ROMs is inferior to the previous DOS-based

GRS software (using this software definitely does not make us feel like children on Christmas morning!). Hopefully the software will improve through its announced "planned future enhancements."

The *Family Finder Index* is included with the *Family Tree Maker for Windows,* a genealogy software program sold by Brøderbund. As mentioned in the previous chapter, Brøderbund also makes the *Family Finder Index* available for free searching on the Internet (Web site: www.familytreemaker.com). Furthermore, the *Family Finder Index* and all its associated CD-ROMs can be purchased separately from the software. (Many of the DOS-based GRS CDs are not readable by the new Windows-based Family Finder Index, and vice-versa.) You'll run across various distributors who sell these CD-ROMs as you visit other genealogy Web sites, for example. As noted, some of these CDs are available in both DOS and Windows versions; others are presently limited to just one or the other format. In general, and especially for the U.S. Census series, the Windows CDs contain much more data per dollar, while the advantage of the DOS CDs is that the included GRS software provides for more versatile searching capabilities. Most Family Archives CDs presently cost in the $20-$50 range, depending on whether they are in Windows or DOS, and on the type and amount of data contained. Considering both the quantity of information per dollar spent and the ease of searching and compiling data, genealogical CD-ROMs do offer some great bargains.

Expansion of Genealogical CD Publishing

Banner Blue is no longer the only publisher of genealogical CD-ROMs. Several other genealogical publishers have already begun, or have announced plans to shortly begin, making selected works available in the CD-ROM format. Some of these contain how-to reference works. Ancestry Incorporated has recently introduced *Ancestry Reference Library,* a CD-ROM collection of five of their most comprehensive guides to major U.S. genealogical repositories, including *The Source: A Guidebook of American Genealogy.*

Everton is another genealogy research firm responsible for producing a CD-ROM. *Family Pedigrees: Everton Publishers, 1500-1990* claims to display some 100,000 family groups, providing name, date, place, and relationship data for about 1 million names (including many duplicates, unfortunately) based on customer-submitted data. While those names are not electronically linked, as in the United Ancestry database, many family links are easily deduced from the data displays.

Other CDs include lots of genealogical data for a given area. Heritage Books, for example, presently offers these collections on CD: The early land, probate, vital, and church records of Hartford, Connecticut (going back to 1635); wills,

Confederate grave registrations, newspaper abstracts, and county histories for nineteenth-century Mississippi; and early New Hampshire genealogical and historical periodicals bundled with an 1874 gazetteer of that state. (Also, the first twenty volumes of, and index to, the periodical *The Virginia Genealogist,* mentioned in Chapter 5, are on CD and sold by this company.) Cost for most such CDs is around $55-$65, or far below what the corresponding hardbound books which contain that same information cost; and all require Windows software.

As with any compiled source, expect some unevenness in quality, especially on CDs which consist of published family histories or of pedigree submissions from individual researchers, such as the Family Archives *World Family Tree* CDs, a continuing Brøderbund-produced series, with each of those CDs containing about 3 million names taken from many thousand pedigree submissions and some other resources.

Volunteer-Produced CD-ROMs

Collaboration between groups and/or individuals has opened a new avenue in the production of genealogy CDs. An excellent example, the *Victorian Pioneers Index,* was compiled by private volunteers working with the government, local genealogical societies, and LDS church officials. More than three hundred volunteers donated 40,000 hours to computerize some 1.8 million births, deaths, and marriages for Victoria, Australia pioneers (1837-88). The state of Tasmania has likewise had its records recently completed, and records for each of the other Australian states are now being assembled; the finished series is expected to include over 5 million names.

Under the direction of local genealogical societies in Great Britain and the LDS Family History Department, the extraction of the 1881 British census has been completed. This project represents the most massive cooperative effort ever undertaken in genealogy. Some 17,000 volunteers donated 2.5 million hours over eight years to extract more than 30 million names. The resulting microfiche indexes are the most detailed, comprehensive, and easy-to-use indexes available. The Family History Department could not commit to a publication date at the time we went to press, but it is hoped that a CD-ROM version of this census will be available in the next couple of years.

In the U.S., participants in the Civil War Soldiers System (CWSS) project have begun entering data from some 5.4 million handwritten records relating to the U.S. Civil War. The project was initiated by the National Park Service and is directed by the Federation of Genealogical Societies and the Civil War Trust (a nonprofit historical group). Many smaller genealogical and historical groups are helping with the project. Upon completion, the CWSS database will list the regiments to which soldiers belonged and battles in which they fought. You can use this database to determine whether an ancestor fought in the Civil War or to learn more about a specific soldier.

The LDS Family History Department designed the data-entry software for the CWSS project, and the Allen County Public Library in Fort Wayne, Indiana, conducted beta tests. The twenty-eight Civil War sites in the National Park Service will maintain copies of the database for public use after the project's first phase is completed, which is expected to be sometime in 1998. The National Archives, LDS Family History Library, and the Internet will also provide access. Future phases of the project include adding pension files and adjutant-general reports to the CWSS database. (If you are interested in volunteering, send your name and address, along with the type of computer you use, to Civil War Index, FGS, P.O. Box 3385, Salt Lake City, UT 84110-3385.)

Afterword

Eco-Genealogy: How and Why to Research the Family Tree Forest

Without an understanding of an ecosystem and the ways in which the parts of that system interact with one another, naturalists can't begin to understand or predict the behavior of whatever portion of the system they wish to study. Similarly, the effectiveness of "eco-genealogical" research is based on the superb predictive value that results from studying any given family as an integral, linked part of its surrounding "family tree forest." Traditional or direct-line genealogy focuses on the ancestral line of a specific person, but many researchers find that a single-minded focus on one person or family imposes blinders that prevent them from finding and using important material. By shifting your focus away from a single family to the extended group, you may be able to view relationships in that family with greater clarity and understanding.

Eco-genealogy does require precise family mapping. Fortunately, besides speeding up research, computers also provide this capability. Software applications not only connect individuals vertically to their ancestors and descendants; they can also represent horizontal relationships (such as siblings or cousins) and diagonal ties (such as aunts, uncles, nieces, and nephews) between relatives, no matter how complicated the pedigree.

By grouping complete, detailed linkages into one nonduplicating system or database, you can accurately recreate the complex forests of your intertwined family trees. We refer to the study of such connected family tree forests as "eco-genealogy." In a completed eco-genealogical database, each person is connected to all of his or her relatives at each possible point of intersection—vertical, horizontal, and diagonal.

By the time this book went to press, we had compiled an eco-genealogy database with some 175,000 individuals within many thousand interlinked family groups. Most of the families in our database are of British descent and resided in, or had some ties to, the colony or state of Virginia, where our research began. A substantial minority lived elsewhere in North America or the Caribbean, or had European origins.

At this point, there are comparably few database names that we consider totally detailed and fully linked (that is, connected to as many relatives and with as many associated names noted as possible). Even in its incomplete state, however, this database increases the effectiveness of our research—and to such a degree as to convince us that a holistic approach to genealogy is much more useful than the traditional approach we used in the past.

Our database grows rapidly because we follow three simple procedures each time we add an individual to the database. First, we compare that person to all other same-named individuals in the database to avoid duplication. Second, we link every name to each known (or sometimes assumed) relative—especially relatives who are already in the database. Finally, within the notes section of each personal record, we list the names of others with whom the individual associated. Doing so provides clues for further research, which helps the database grow even more quickly—the more names assembled, the greater the likelihood that we will be able to use those clues to extend the database.

Advantages of Eco-Genealogy

Without an awareness of the term "eco-genealogy," many of you have already discovered the wisdom of broadening your research. To achieve the more inclusive, accurate, and productive view that eco-genealogy provides, you simply need to extend your study outward from any individual. Include siblings, in-laws, aunts, uncles, cousins, and even close friends and neighbors. Initially the group may seem loosely related, but as you progress you will find multiple links that bind individuals and families more tightly.

For example, child-naming and marriage patterns of American colonists and other North American settlers often reveal family structures. Many children were given names reflecting their family heritage. By studying names in a sibling group, then referring to facts about related families, you can often deduce parental and/or ancestral identity.

As we have studied marriage patterns among this group, we've found that most pre-twentieth-century families were highly in-bred; marriages among in-laws, step-siblings, and even blood relatives—especially cousins—were common. While interfamily marriages created complex, interlinked family groups, these links tended to remain within traditional and somewhat predictable bounds. Thus, spouse surnames in the British section of the International Genealogical Index (IGI) for sixteenth- and seventeenth-century emigrants often reappear in the eighteenth and nineteenth centuries as the emigrants' descendants in North America continued to marry into the same related families. Computer linking enables tracking of these marriage patterns and precise mapping of the resulting tangled relationships.

By including in your database all families related by marriage or blood, you increase the database's value considerably, since so many individuals married within this expanded gene pool. Often you can surmise in-law families from this store of data, which can help you determine surnames and ancestry that you have been unable to identify previously for maternal lines.

In addition to helping you use naming and marriage patterns to determine relationships, eco-genealogy offers the following advantages:

- **Enables better use of circumstantial evidence:** An eco-genealogical approach encourages greater use of circumstantial evidence. You can test all possible identities or relationships that logically explain evidence, since your wrong guesses will be winnowed out and correct ones confirmed as your research continues. You expand the database by using every fact you can find and searching for logical links to those facts, even if you can't verify the connections. Inferred links provide the only route for taking research forward for some families, especially in areas such as the southern U.S., where many records were destroyed and information is often difficult to substantiate.

- **Illuminates and prevents mistakes:** Because the evidence we gather is sometimes sketchy and unsubstantiated, we inevitably make mistakes in our linking experiments. However, as our database expands, these mistakes are revealed. When a particular piece of data contradicts other information, we re-examine the links to determine the problem and make revisions. Discovering and correcting these linking errors becomes easier as the database grows. The more valid connections we establish between family members, the more remote become our chances of making linking errors in that family.

- **Provides evidence for family links:** Family links that are invisible in a single family tree usually appear at a more inclusive level. Therefore, even if you can find no data for a person or family, you are not necessarily stymied. By tracing the individual or family in the context of the larger family system, you may overcome—or at least be able to work around—the considerable handicap of missing records.

Effective Eco-Genealogical Research

Regardless of whether you have a computerized eco-genealogy database, you can help your research progress by following three basic rules of eco-genealogy: First, scrupulously avoid duplication; second, consider every piece of data in context; and third, cooperate with other researchers.

- **Avoid duplication:** By duplicating information, you lose the considerable advantages of interlinking. Yet even experienced genealogists can't always determine if the name that appears in one record represents the same individual as the identical name in another record. Databases present the same challenge: Often it is difficult to determine whether similar entries are duplicates that should be merged, or if they actually refer to two individuals with the same name. Fortunately, as your database expands, you'll eventually gain sufficient evidence to resolve identity questions.

- **Context is everything:** As they study ecological and biological details within a narrow focus, naturalists must constantly remain aware of relevant events in the infringing environment. Likewise, genealogists must maintain a double focus to recognize clues wherever they appear, because circumstantial evidence can surface in the most unexpected places. For example, we have solved research problems based on circumstantial evidence that we have discovered in records as many as seven or eight generations removed from the original problem, and even in records from different states, provinces, and countries.

- **Cooperate with other researchers:** Just as a rock thrown into a pool sends ripples through the entire body of water, each family discovery affects our understanding of each related family. Practically every piece of data, verified line, or even inferred relationship makes possible a growing circle of discoveries. Only through sharing family facts and discoveries with other research can the outward expansion of that circle continue.

Assembling all facts about all families into one nonduplicating, worldwide system would, of course, provide maximum eco-genealogical benefits. This is the goal of the GenWeb, mentioned at the end of Chapter 11. As increasing numbers of knowledgeable genealogists post data to the GenWeb, and as quality interactive software evolves, the process of correcting mistakes and establishing links will become easier and faster. By encouraging genealogists to establish links between databases that contain the same names, the GenWeb already provides the means and motivation for genealogists to make corrections and eliminate duplicates.

Assembling and correctly linking all known data and reasonable suppositions into a single, accurate, global family tree is the ultimate goal of all genealogical research. Until recently, such an ideal was too overwhelming to consider seriously, much less achieve. With the GenWeb, that potential now exists.

Collaboration with Allied Fields

When genealogists cooperate more fully with allied disciplines such as genetics and demography, the possibilities will be limitless. These fields, after all, share an interest in humanity's inheritance and examine the same subject, albeit from differing viewpoints—genetics from a micro-view (DNA encoded on the human gene), genealogy from a mid-view (DNA transmitted through families), and demography from a macro-view (DNA transmitted through populations). Collaboration will certainly benefit each of these disciplines.

The Internet provides a powerful means for such collaboration. Medical researchers working to identify chromosome and gene locations of inherited diseases have already begun some genealogical collaboration. Geneticists are also beginning to use genealogy to further their research. For example, Dr. Thomas Roderick at the Center for Human Genetics in Bar Harbor, Maine, recently conducted a study to better analyze mitochondrial DNA (mtDNA) structure. As part of the study, he asked readers of certain genealogy publications to submit matrilineal pedigrees (charts that trace the female line, daughter to mother); he received more than 350 responses. He will use mtDNA analysis to verify the accuracy of the pedigrees.

This study provides a glimpse of the possibilities of biologically-based genealogical verification. The ability to prove descent through means other than just written records would revolutionize genealogy. Imagine how useful an all-inclusive Internet eco-genealogy database, such as a mature version of the GenWeb, could be for large-scale and in-depth DNA studies—especially if this database was used in conjunction with geneticists' ambitious genome map project.

Conclusion

Computer technology has the potential to show us the forest surrounding each of our family trees. Certainly computers are just tools, but they are tools that enable us to deal adequately with the basic units of our field: Family links. These relationships dynamically bind our families, our extended families, and the entire human family into one interdependent whole. Exploiting this technology to reconstruct the genealogy of humanity presents an exciting opportunity for genealogists to unite their efforts, but also an awesome challenge—most of us, after all, are just learning what it means to cooperate online! Fortunately, adopting the holistic view and cooperative stance of eco-genealogy provides a productive way to combine our genealogical skills and technological capabilities for the benefit of all.

Appendix A

Soundex Search

(This section was abridged and extracted from the National Archives publication *The 1790–1890 Federal Population Censuses: Catalog of National Archives Microfilm*, National Archives Trust Fund Board, Washington, D.C., 1979.)

The Soundex is a phonetic index, not a strictly alphabetical one. It codes surnames based on sound rather than spelling. For example, surnames that sound the same but are spelled differently, such as Smith and Smyth, have the same code and are indexed together.

The steps we've outlined below apply to the Soundex for U.S. census records from 1880, 1900, 1910, and 1920, and the Miracode (a variation of Soundex) for 1910.

Table A-1. Soundex Coding Guide

Number in Code	Letters Represented
1	B, P, F, V
2	C, S, K, G, J, Q, X, Z
3	D, T
4	L
5	M, N
6	R

Step 1: Code Surname

Every Soundex code consists of a letter and three numbers, such as B-536. The letter is always the first letter of the surname, whether it is a vowel or a consonant; the numbers represent the next three consonants of the surname—not including H, W, or Y—according to the coding guide in Table A-1 (note the exceptions discussed later). If there are not three consonants following the first letter of the surname, zeroes complete the three-digit code;

for example, the surname Lee is represented by L-000. Most surnames can be coded using the table above; however, some names contain letter combinations or other features that require special instructions.

- **Prefixes:** If the surname has a prefix (for example, D', De, dela, Di, du, Le, van, Von), it may be listed under a code either with or without the prefix, so you should search for both. The surname vanDevanter, for example, could be V-531 or D-153. (Mc and Mac are not considered prefixes and should be coded like other surnames.)

- **Double letters:** If the surname contains double letters, you should treat them as one letter. For example, in the surname Lloyd, the second "l" should be crossed out, making the code L-300. In the surname Gutierrez, the second "r" should be disregarded, so the code is G-362.

- **Side-by-side letters:** A surname may have different side-by-side letters that receive the same number on the Soundex coding guide. For example, the "c," "k," and "s" in Jackson all receive a number 2 code. Adjacent letters with the same code should be regarded as only one letter, so Jackson is coded J-250. This rule applies to the first letter of the surname as well, even though it isn't coded: The "Pf" in Pfister would receive a number 1 code for both the "p" and "f." The "p" becomes the code letter, and the "f" is disregarded because it has the same code number as "p," so the code would be P-236.

- **Native American and Asian names:** Phonetically spelled Native American or Asian names have sometimes been coded as if they are one continuous name. For example, the code for the name Dances with Wolves may be D-522 (Dances) or W-412 (Wolves); the code for the name Shinka-Wa-Sa may be S-520 (Shinka) or S-000 (Sa).

- **Single-term names:** Many people, especially Alaskans and Native Americans, used only a single name, such as Loksi or Hiawatha, rather than both a first and last name. Their descendants may not have added surnames until as late as the twentieth century. You may need to code such a name as though it were a surname.

Table A-2. Abbreviations Used in the Soundex

Relationships to Head of Household	
A	Aunt
AdD	Adopted daughter

Relationships to Head of Household	
AdS	Adopted son
At	Attendant
B	Brother
BL	Brother-in-law
Bo	Boarder
C	Cousin
D	Daughter
DL	Daughter-in-law
F	Father
FB	Foster brother
FF	Foster father
FL	Father-in-law
FM	Foster mother
FSi	Foster sister
GA	Great Aunt
GD	Granddaughter
GF	Grandfather
GGF	Great-grandfather
GGM	Great-grandmother
GGGF	Great-great-grandfather
GGGM	Great-great-grandmother
GM	Grandmother
GN	Grand nephew
GNi	Grand niece
GS	Grandson

Relationships to Head of Household	
GU	Great Uncle
Hh	Hired hand
Hm	Hired man
I	Inmate
L	Lodger
M	Mother
ML	Mother-in-law
N	Nephew
Ni	Niece
Nu	Nurse
O	Officer
P	Patient
Pa	Partner (share common abode)
Pr	Prisoner
Pri	Principal
Pu	Pupil
R	Roomer
S	Son
SB	Step-brother
SBL	Step-brother-in-law
SD	Step-daughter
SDL	Step-daughter-in-law
Se	Servant
SF	Step-father
SFL	Step-father-in-law

Relationships to Head of Household	
Si	Sister
SiL	Sister-in-law
SL	Son-in-law
SM	Step-mother
SML	Step-mother-in-law
SS	Step-son
SSi	Step-sister
SSiL	Step-sister-in-law
SSL	Step-son-in-law
Su	Superintendent
U	Uncle
W	Wife
Wa	Warden
Citizenship Status	
A	Alien
NA	Naturalized
PA	First papers filed

Step 2: Find Soundex Roll

Coded surnames and other data are recorded on 2,367 microfilm rolls, which are listed in *The 1790–1890 Federal Population Censuses: Catalog of National Archives Microfilm* alphabetically by state (includes territories also). After you've coded the surname, you must know or speculate the place of residence of the individual, family, or institution for the appropriate census year. In the microfilm roll lists, the Soundex codes are arranged alphabetically by the first letter of the surname, then chronologically by code numbers. Table A-3 shows this arrangement for the first few rolls for Pennsylvania. In this table, key features discussed below appear in brackets.

Table A-3. Sample List of Soundex Rolls for Pennsylvania, 1880

Microfilm Roll Number	Soundex Codes for Surname (First Initials in Parentheses)
1	A-000 thru A-351
2	A-352 thru A-450 (K)
...	
14	B-600 thru B-620 (J)
15	B-620 (J) thru B-624
16	B-625 thru B-630
17	B-631 thru B-640 (F)
18	B-640 (G) thru B-650 (Q)
19	B-650 (R) thru B-652
20	B-653 thru B-666
21	C-000 thru C-200 (I)
22	C-200 (J) thru C-316 [*this is the code range for Cook, Levi*]

You should match your Soundex code with a range specified in *The 1790–1890 Federal Population Censuses: Catalog of National Archives Microfilm.* Table A-3 references the code C-200, which applies to Cook and similar surnames. Rolls 21 and 22 include cards with this code. Often there are so many cards with the same codes that all of them can't fit on a single microfilm roll, so some cards must be included with the next roll. In the Soundex listings, capital letters in parentheses indicate a break in the cards. A letter in parentheses at the far right of a roll listing indicates that the last card on the roll is for a person whose first name begins with that letter. The letter after the first code on the next roll is the first initial of the person listed on the first card. For example, roll 21 of Pennsylvania's Soundex ends with C-200, and the last card contains information for someone whose first or middle name begins with "I." Roll 22 continues with the code C-200, beginning with the initial "J." If you were searching for a Soundex card for Levi Cook, you would begin with roll 22 of T-769. Obviously, to find some names you may need to consult more than one microfilm roll.

Step 3: Identify the Correct Soundex Card

Soundex microfilm rolls include four types of cards: Family Cards, Other Members of Family—Continued Cards, Individual Cards, and Institution Cards. On the microfilm rolls, divider cards usually note the beginning of a new Soundex code. Beneath the coded surname at the top left of each Soundex card, you'll find the surname and first name of the head of household. (Census schedules did not require a middle name or initial.) Surnames are arranged by Soundex code, and first names are generally arranged alphabetically. When you find a relevant Family Card, you should record the following information: State or territory; volume, ED (Enumerator District) sheet, and line numbers; and county, city, and MCD (Minor Civil Division, as in wards, precincts, districts, etc.). This information is pertinent for subsequent research steps. Key data on Levi Cook's card is Pennsylvania; volume 82, ED 21, sheet 8, line 15; and Somerset County, Shade [Township].

Frequently, Soundex codes may appear on the cards in a random, nonconsecutive list; for example, M-200 followed by M-190, M-205, and M-189. In these instances (usually noted by divider cards), disregard the codes and focus on the alphabetized given names and initials. If you do find cards with mixed codes, you may need to consult more than one microfilm roll. If you exhaust these options without finding a pertinent Soundex card, try various spellings of the surname and new codings, or explore ED descriptions and maps.

If you cannot find a name in the first three types of Soundex cards, consider the fourth type, Institution Cards, which appear at the end of the last roll of Soundex microfilm for each state or territory. For example, roll 168 of Pennsylvania's Soundex includes "Y-630 thru Institutions." Unlike the other cards, the Institution Cards are arranged alphabetically by the name of the institution. They exclude personal data on individuals, but they include jurisdictional data (state, county, city, and ED, and often street and house numbers) that will help you find the correct census schedules. If you suspect that an individual lived in an institution, you can use the Institution Cards to find the schedule without looking at the other types of cards.

Step 4: Find Microfilmed Schedule

After recording pertinent data from a Soundex card, consult the section of *The 1790–1890 Federal Population Censuses: Catalog of National Archives Microfilm* that pertains to the census records you wish to find; for example, "Tenth Census of the United States, 1880." The catalog lists the states, District of Columbia, and territories alphabetically. You'll find the number of the microfilm rolls at the far left, then a description of what they cover. The microfilm cites counties and often cities within the state alphabetically; within large urban areas, MCDs such as wards may also be numbered, then listed alphabetically. The catalog also notes EDs, often in numerical order. For example, in T-9 (the 1880 census), rolls 1190–1194 pertain to Pennsylvania's Schuylkill County, EDs 1–128. Frequently, the catalog notes rolls that include certain sheets for an ED or other jurisdiction. You should match the county, city, MCD, ED, and sheet number on the Soundex card with the information or range in the catalog. The number to the left of that information designates the microfilm roll number of the appropriate census.

Step 5: Locate ED, Sheet, and Line Numbers on Schedule

At the beginning of each microfilm roll, you'll see a large, handwritten number, such as "T-9, 1195." Use this number to confirm that you are viewing the appropriate microfilm publication. A volume page indicates the coverage of the schedules. (Some rolls have additional volume pages throughout the roll.) Because some volume pages contain inaccurate information about EDs or other jurisdictions, you'll need to scan carefully the roll preceding or following the one that appears to be correct. Following the volume page, the schedules generally are arranged in the order stated in the catalog. Enumerators usually recorded the city, county, state, and ward or other MCD on the front of the schedule. Handwritten ED numbers are on the upper left side, on the third line, under the line marked "Supervisor's District." Match the sheet number from the Soundex card to the page number of the first line on the upper left side of the schedule. On the card for Levi Cook, for example, the sheet number is 9, which corresponds to the number on the census schedule. Handwritten numbers on the schedules ordinarily start at 1 in each ED and run consecutively on each sheet, A–D. (Disregard the stamped numbers that appear at the right side of the schedules.) Use the line number on the Soundex card to match the name or institution on the card with census entries; for example, the Soundex card for Levi Cook notes line 15, and Levi Cook's entry appears on line 15 of the census schedule.

Appendix B

Calendar Changes

In March 1582, Pope Gregory XIII abolished the Julian calendar in favor of the calendar that bears his name. Rome, Spain, and Portugal began conforming to the new calendar on October 4, 1582; France made the switch on December 9, 1582; the Catholic states of Germany changed to the new calendar in 1583; and Scotland complied on January 1, 1600. Denmark, Sweden, and the Protestant German states adopted the reformed calendar in or around 1700. Britain and its colonies began using the Gregorian calendar on September 2, 1752. Russia kept the Julian calendar until 1917, when the czars were overthrown and the Soviet government was established.

In terms of genealogical research, the Gregorian calendar caused two important changes. First, eleven days were added to the date on which the calendar was adopted; people born before and still living after the change may have added eleven days to their birth dates. For instance, George Washington was born February 11, 1732, but we celebrate his birthday eleven days later, on February 22. Second, with the Gregorian calendar, the new year begins on January 1, rather than on March 25, which marked the Julian new year. This change has proven significant for genealogists because it was anticipated in some areas and resisted in others; dates that fell between January 1 and March 25 were often written in a "double-dating" fashion, in which the Julian date is recorded first, followed by the Gregorian date; for example, 23 Mar 1729/30, or 16 Jan 1750–1.

These factors occasionally create confusion—for example, a will dated September 1680 might have been proved in February 1680; or a couple could have a marriage date of April 9, 1747, while their first child, born eleven months after the wedding, could have a recorded birth date of March 9, 1747. Also, because the Julian calendar year began in March, the switch to the new calendar changed the numerical designations of the months; that is, March became the third month, and January became the first month. September, for example, was the seventh month on the old calendar and was often abbreviated "7-ber" or "7-bre" or "VII-bre." After the change it became the ninth month.

Appendix C

National Archives Regional System

National Archives—New England
Region
380 Trapelo Road
Waltham, MA 02154

National Archives—Pittsfield Region
100 Dan Fox Drive
Pittsfield, MA 01201

National Archives—Northeast Region
201 Varick Street
New York, NY 10014

National Archives—Mid-Atlantic
Region
9th and Market Streets, Room 1350
Philadelphia, PA 19107

National Archives—Southeast Region
1557 St. Joseph Avenue
East Point, GA 30344

National Archives—Great Lakes
Region
7358 South Pulaski Rd
Chicago, IL 60629

National Archives—Central Plains
Region
2306 East Bannister Road
Kansas City, MO 64131

National Archives—Southwest Region
501 West Felix St.
P.O. Box 6216
Fort Worth, TX 76115

National Archives—Rocky Mountain
Region
Bldg. 48, Denver Federal Center
P.O. Box 25307
Denver, CO 80225

National Archives—Pacific Southwest
Region
24000 Avila Road
Laguna Niguel, CA 92656

National Archives—Pacific Sierra
Region
1000 Commodore Drive
San Bruno, CA 94066

National Archives—Pacific Northwest
Region
6125 Sand Point Way NE
Seattle, WA 98115

National Archives—Alaska Region
654 West Third Avenue
Anchorage, AK 99501

GLOSSARY: Computer Terms

Archie A computer service for locating files available to the public on the Internet.

ARPANET Advanced Research Projects Agency Network, created in 1969 by the U.S. Department of Defense. This network was the precursor to the Internet.

ASCII (pronounced ask'ee) The standard code used for information exchange among communication devices. Every common text character (letters and numbers), and several special computer control characters, are coded through a unique binary number.

ASCII file A file containing only ASCII characters. Most programs of value to genealogists can utilize ASCII files.

backup files Duplicate files you prepare by copying your original files to another disk. Backup files should be prepared regularly for all your important information in case of a serious computer malfunction or other disaster. Backup files should be stored in a separate location.

baud A measure of data transmission speed.

BBS Bulletin Board System. Electronic message posting areas that are accessible via a telephone line.

bit BInary DigiT. The smallest unit of information processed by a computer.

BITNET A cooperative computer network begun by IBM and the university community in 1981; recently merged with CREN (Computer Research & Education Network). BITNET supports e-mail and file transfer.

Boolean logic A type of formal logic formulated by George Boole and used in information retrieval to specify a search for information by using common words such as "AND," "OR," and "NOT." For example, to find information dealing with Smiths who married Joneses but not Joneses who lived in New York, a Boolean search command might be something like this: Search Smith AND (Jones NOT New York).

bps Bits per second. A measure of data transmission speed.

buffer A memory area or electronic register where data is held temporarily until it can be processed.

bug A glitch or problem with a software application.

byte A sequence of eight bits that the computer interprets as a single unit (e.g., a number, letter, special code).

CD-ROM (Compact Disk-Read-Only Memory) A portable disk that stores data used by a computer (e.g., graphic images, programs, files).

chip A silicon wafer on which is etched an integrated electronic circuit made up of thousands of microscopic transistors.

client A computer that is attached to a computer network and that requests services from a network server.

computer An electronic machine that can perform numerous complex logical or arithmetic operations.

CPU Central Processing Unit. Main processing unit of a computer.

cursor A line or square of light displayed on your monitor that indicates where the next computer operation (for example, a keystroke) will have its effect. If you press a letter key on the keyboard, the letter is displayed at the location of the cursor, and the cursor moves forward one space.

database program A software application designed to organize numbers or text into a series of records. Information is stored in a field, and a record can be made up of several fields. In turn, a series of related records are collected into a database file. Records in a database file may be searched and sorted, and specific records selected for viewing or printing.

directory A list of files on a disk.

disk drive A device installed in or attached to a computer used to store information or applications on a magnetic disk.

diskette A flexible, specially coated portable disk on which you can save electronic data.

DNS Domain Name System. A database system on the Internet that translates domain names into the numeric addresses. The DNS enables you to communicate with others on the network without having to remember long lists of numbers.

domain name An Internet address that consists of a hierarchical sequence of names separated by periods, from the most specific to the most general (e.g., johndoe@vtvm1.cc.vt.edu).

DOS Disk Operating System. A generic term to refer to operating systems that use commands rather than having a graphical user interface (GUI). The most common of these are DR DOS, MS-DOS, and PC DOS.

dot matrix printer A printer that uses a printhead (much like the traveling type ball on some brands of typewriters) with 9 or 24 small movable pins. Different combinations of pins hitting an inked ribbon produce the character sent to the printer from the computer.

download To transfer a file to your computer from another computer via a telephone line.

e-mail Electronic mail. Electronic messages sent or received via a computer network.

export To save a file created in one application to another in a different, compatible application.

FidoNet An international bulletin board network carrying a variety of genealogical message areas. (See also BBS.)

freenet A network set up by grassroots efforts to supply Internet services to a local, urban area. Access is provided either through the public libraries or by dialing in.

freeware Software available to computer users at no charge and available through many electronic bulletin boards, computer clubs, and computer interest groups.

FTP File Transfer Protocol. A high-level protocol used to transfer files from one computer to another on the Internet. FTP is often used as a verb to describe the transfer of files using this protocol.

gateway A hardware/software package that connects two networks by allowing incompatible protocols to communicate.

GEDCOM GEnealogical Data COMmunications. An application used to format genealogical data for access and exchange. GEDCOM was developed by the Family History Department of The Church of Jesus Christ of Latter-day Saints to provide a standardized way of entering genealogical information.

GUI Graphical User Interface. A presentation on the computer monitor that is illustrated with icons and other graphic representations to assist users in performing tasks.

hard disk A disk within the CPU that stores data and software applications.

host computer A computer attached to a network that provides services to many other computers simultaneously.

hypertext A method of linking information through the use of key words. Hypertext provides immediate access to related information about a key word.

import To retrieve a file created in one application into another compatible application.

ink jet printer A printer that uses small jets of ink to create characters and images. Printed pages are similar in quality to those produced by a laser printer.

Internet A collection of networks and gateways including local, regional, and national networks that share the same addressing scheme, telecommunications protocol, and services (e-mail, remote login, file transfer, etc.).

IP/TCP Internet Protocol/Transmission Control Protocol. A protocol suite used to move information through dissimilar networks on the Internet.

IP address The numeric address of any computer connected to the Internet.

kilobyte KB. A unit of measure for memory or disk storage capacity. 1,024 bytes.

laser printer A printer that utilizes laser technology to print text or images on a photo-sensitive drum, and transfers the information from the drum to paper. Produces the highest quality of printed documentation.

listservers Electronic discussions conducted by e-mail over BITNET using LISTSERV protocols. Similar lists are available on the Internet, often using the UNIX readnews (rn) feature.

megabyte MB. A unit of measure for memory or disk storage capacity. 1,048,576 bytes.

modem MOdulator/DEModulator. A device used to convert digital signals of the computer to analog signals used on telephone lines and vice versa.

monitor A device similar to your television set, and attached to a computer to display information. Used in conjunction with a mouse or keyboard, it allows you to interact with the computer.

MS-DOS The acronym for Microsoft Disk Operating System, a computer operating system produced by Microsoft Corporation.

network A system that sends and receives data and messages, typically over a cable. A network enables multiple computers to communicate with each other.

node Any device (computer, modem, etc.) that is attached to a network and is capable of communicating with other network devices.

NREN National Research and Education Network. A U.S. government high-speed computer network linking national and regional networks; built on the backbone network NSFnet.

OCR Optical Character Recognition. A technology whereby characters on a printed page are read by a mechanical device (scanner) into a computer by using an OCR program.

online The condition in which your computer is connected to another computer. Typically used to describe your connection to a BBS.

OS/2 A computer operating system marketed by IBM Corporation.

packet The unit of information by which the network communicates. Electronic messages are broken into packets, which travel independently and are reassembled at the receiving node.

parallel A type of electrical connection that uses eight wires and is capable of carrying eight bits of a byte simultaneously. Most commonly used to connect printers to computers.

port A specialized plug on a computer that allows you to connect a peripheral device (such as a printer) to the computer.

protocol A set of rules that allows computers to connect with one another.

public-domain software Non-copyrighted software.

RAM Random Access Memory. A type of computer memory that enables random access to various portions of information stored either in the computer or on a disk.

remote access The ability to access a computer from beyond its physical location. It requires communications hardware, software, and some physical link, such as telephone lines or Telnet login.

ROM Read-Only Memory. A type of computer memory from which the computer can read information, but to which new information cannot be saved.

ROM is generally used to store configuration information the computer needs when you turn it on.

scanner An optical device used to read characters or illustrations on a printed page.

serial A type of electrical connection used to send the eight bits of a byte one at a time in a series.

server A networked computer that is capable of recognizing and responding to client requests for services, from basic print services to support for complex database systems.

shareware Software applications freely distributed through the public domain, but for which you should pay if you use regularly.

SIG Special Interest Group. BBS that focuses on a specific topic.

software Computer programs and data that can be installed on the computer using diskettes or CD-ROMs.

sysop Systems Operator. An individual who controls and operates an electronic bulletin board or some node on a network. You should contact the sysop if you have questions about that system.

telecommunications Any technology used to exchange using telephone lines.

teleconferencing A form of telecommunications in which individuals at various locations may take part in the same conference.

Telnet A protocol that allows a computer to interact with a remote computer on a network as if the two were directly connected to each other.

Tiny Tafel A computer genealogy file format that contains names, places, and dates, and can help you find other researchers interested in your family names.

UNIX An operating system developed by AT&T Bell Laboratories. It allows a computer to handle multiple users and applications simultaneously.

USENET A worldwide news conferencing system available through various networks. Its newsgroup soc_roots provides articles on genealogy.

user group An organization composed of individuals with a common interest in a particular type of computer or software.

user ID Name or identification number that identifies a user to a host computer. For example, before you can use an electronic bulletin board you must enter a previously assigned user ID.

virus A program that can be transferred from one computer to another, corrupting data and operations.

word processor A type of software application designed for writing, revising, or deleting text.

GLOSSARY: Legal Terms

administration/administrator/administratrix The process of collecting, managing, and distributing an estate. When the person responsible for this process is chosen by the court (as happens when the decedent leaves no will, or when the person chosen as the executor declines to accept that office), that person is known as the administrator (if male) or administratrix (if female). Normally he or she must enter into a bond with sureties; bondsmen are often relations.

affinity Relationship through marriage rather than blood.

age of discretion Under the old English common law, between age twelve and eighteen for females and age fourteen and twenty-one for males.

antenuptial agreement A contract made before marriage by the bride- and groom-to-be setting forth their property rights. Usually (not always) made before second marriages to protect the property of children born in previous marriages; most common among the Dutch in New Netherlands, and in community property states.

attorney Anyone authorized to act on behalf of another.

beneficiary One who inherits property, or anyone for whom a trust is created or who receives a property benefit.

bequeath (bequest) To dispose of personal property by will. Also, property received through will.

by representation See *per stipes*.

by these presents Reference to the document in which this phrase occurs.

chattel Animate or inanimate personal property; in earlier times often used as a synonym for slaves.

child of tender years Under the age of discretion.

circuit court See *court of probate*.

community property Property obtained by husband, wife, or both, that the law considers jointly owned. Applies in Arizona, California, Idaho, Louisiana, Nevada, New Mexico, Texas, and Washington. See *cotenancy*.

consanguinity Blood relationship.

consideration The price (or other motive) in a contract.

consort Spouse (archaic).

conveyance See *deed.*

corporeal property Visible property (e.g., a house).

cotenancy Joint ownership. There are four types: community property, tenancy by the entirety, joint tenancy, and tenancy in common (see individual entries).

county court See *court of probate.*

court of probate A court having jurisdiction of probate matters.

court of the ordinary See *court of probate.*

curtesy In common-law states, the estate to which a man is entitled upon the death of his wife.

decedent A deceased person.

deed (or **conveyance**) The document that transfers title in real property. Most common are the deed in fee and warranty deed. Others are quitclaim deeds, trust deeds, deeds of release, deeds of partition, and gift deeds.

deposition Written testimony, taken under oath.

devise An individual's real property.

devisee One who receives real property (devise) by means of a will.

devisor One who gives his/her real property (devise) by means of a will.

district court See *court of probate.*

dower (**endowment**) Under common law, property from a man's estate to which his widow has claim (traditionally one-third). Setting off, or assigning, the dower is referred to as an endowment.

endowment See *dower.*

escheat Property reversion to the state when no heirs are qualified.

et uxor Latin term meaning "and wife." Often abbreviated *et ux.*

executor/executrix The person appointed by the testator to carry out will provisions.

fee simple Total ownership.

folio A leaf, as in a book. In older records, folio may refer to both sides of a leaf (i.e., two pages), or occasionally to more than two pages.

guardian The person assigned the responsibility to care for another person's rights and property. A guardian is chosen, or elected, by a child who is of the age of discretion or is appointed by the court. A guardian (often the mother or step-mother) was commonly named when only the father was deceased. Less commonly, a father may have been appointed guardian to his own child (e.g., when he was made trustee for property the child had inherited from a maternal grandparent).

heir One who inherits property or position upon the death of another (usually a relative).

incorporeal property Unseen property (e.g., rent). (See also *corporeal property.*)

indenture Reciprocal agreement signed by both parties. Many colonial immigrants came as indentured servants, meaning their passage and other items were paid for by a master whom they agreed to serve for a stated period (often seven years).

infant A minor; one who has not attained legal age.

instrument A legal document.

intermarriage A reciprocally agreed marriage contract.

intestate A deceased person who did not leave a will. (See also *testate.*)

issue All lineal, or direct, descendants (e.g., children, grandchildren, great-grandchildren).

item Latin term meaning "likewise" or "also." Often used to mark divisions or paragraphs in wills.

joint tenancy Joint land ownership with rights of survivorship. Joint tenancy can be terminated whenever any of the parties sells. (See also *cotenancy* and *tenancy by the entirety.*)

lease An agreement transferring real property, usually for a specified time period, thus creating a landlord-tenant relationship.

legacy (legatee/legator) A gift of personal property by will. The person who wills the legacy is the legator, and the person who receives the legacy is the legatee.

legal age Adulthood; under English common law, twenty-one for males, eighteen for females.

lien A claim by someone upon another's property as security to pay a debt.

life estate An estate lasting only for the life of the person given it, as in the case of a dower estate.

moiety Half.

mortgage A conditional title transfer of real property, as security to pay a debt. Under common law, the mortgagee has land possession rights; this has now been changed in many states.

natural affection Legal term often used in conveyances between near relatives, when no or little money is involved (e.g., when a parent grants property to a child).

ordinary A judicial probate officer in Georgia (and, formerly, in South Carolina and Texas). Also, a hostelry where food and drink could be sold, requiring the keeper to receive an ordinary license. Records of the latter are often found in court-order books.

orphan A minor or infant who has lost one or both parents.

orphans' court See *court of probate*.

per stipes A Latin term used in wills to indicate that the estate is to be divided among a group of children who will be given the same share their ancestor would have received if the ancestor was living. Today the term "by representation" is more commonly used.

petition A non-suit request for court action.

power of attorney A document that gives authority to one person to act on behalf of another.

probate To prove (as in, to prove a will). Also, all records relating to the settling of an estate.

quitrent A token payment (similar to a tax payment) discharging the tenant from other rents (archaic).

real property (**realty**) Land, as opposed to personal property (personality).

release A document giving up to another a person's right to something. For instance, if a man sold property in a common-law state, his wife had to sign a Release of Dower to relinquish her dower rights.

relict Widow or widower (archaic).

security A person who legally promises to pay if another defaults his or her obligations.

separate examination The legally required questioning of a married woman by a court official, as in granting a deed in which her dower rights must be relinquished, for instance.

surety See *security*.

surrender To give up a lease before it expires.

surrogate court See *court of probate*.

tenancy in common Concurrent land ownership by separate titles. Owners claim no rights of survivorship, and any party can terminate tenancy. (See also *cotenancy*.)

tenancy by the entirety Joint land ownership by spouses with rights of survivorship. Most states no longer allow this, unless specifically stated in a legal document. (See also *cotenancy*.)

testable Capable of making a will.

testate Having made or left a valid will.

testator/testatrix A person who has died leaving a valid will.

testes Latin term meaning "witness;" sometimes abbreviated *test*.

trustee The legal caretaker of property held in trust for another's benefit.

Index

W